A Year With Symfony

Writing healthy, reusable Symfony2 code

Matthias Noback

A Year With Symfony

Writing healthy, reusable Symfony2 code

Matthias Noback

This book is for sale at http://www.lulu.com/content/paperback/a-year-with-symfony/14090903

This version was published on 2014-08-01

ISBN 978-90-821201-1-0

To Liesbeth and Lucas, because this is... Life

Contents

Foreword

By *Luis Cordova*

Open source projects have a history and a lot of reasoning behind them that evolves. Symfony2 has been evolving for the past several years. Many new developers coming to use the framework feel the steep curve of mastering the framework and overcome it at the end, but are left with many doubts when it comes to developing their projects in the true Symfony way.

For symfony1 there was a book that covered the symfony1 practices. For Symfony2 there is the Book which is the major source for documentation. The Book has also Cookbook entries which help somewhat. However, even then not all the aspects and practices brewed during so many years can be summarized with those resources for developers with a hunger for understanding the why's and best practices that only real-life field experience with Symfony can provide. There are blogs about Symfony development also, however they are sparse and blogs even like mine assume a lot of things about the readership and are more for experimental things and nuances of the framework. What has been missing up to now has been a strong technical opinion poured in a book catering to the community and pointing in the right "Symfony way".

Matthias has had more than one year understanding Symfony from the inside out and bringing responses to the why's to the surface for us. I could not trust anyone other than a Certified Symfony Developer to do this. Seldom times have I felt I understood Symfony so well to use it as my very own arsenal. Reading this book has been one of those times. Another time was when I heard Kris Wallsmith explaining/acting out the Symfony Security Component. This book is a must for everyone who is eager to carefully understand the framework.

Matthias will give away in this book a lot of secrets so you will find yourself often coming back to the book to see how a recommendation was issued, and what to do in your case. Matthias has also spoken about things I even did not think I would find in this book and he did it in a straightforward manner with examples and code.

I truly hope you enjoy this book.

Your friend from the symfony community,
Luis Cordova (@cordoval)

Introduction

A year with Symfony. In fact, for me it's been *more* than a year, almost 6 years even. First with symfony 1 (mind the lower case and the separate 1), then with Symfony2. Symfony2 is what you may call a "mature" framework. You can do pretty advanced things with it. And when you want to do one of these very advanced things, you can also choose not to install the entire framework, but just one of its components.

Starting to work with Symfony2 meant for me: learning much about programming in general and applying many of the things I only knew from books to any code I produced from then on. Symfony2 did this for me: encourage me to do things right.

In the meantime, I've written a lot about Symfony2, contributed to its documentation (specifically some Cookbook articles and the documentation for the Security Component and the Config Component), I started my own blog[1] with articles about PHP in general, Symfony2, its components and related frameworks and libraries like Silex and Twig. And I became a Symfony2 Certified Developer, during the very first exam session in Paris at the Symfony Live conference in 2012.

All this is now being followed by the book you're reading now, called *A Year With Symfony*. It contains many of the best practices that me and my fellow developers at IPPZ[2] discovered while working on large Symfony2 applications. It also contains some in-depth knowledge that you'll need to have when you're going one step further than just writing code inside a controller or a template.

Thank you

Before I continue, let me take a moment to thank some people who have helped me finishing this book. First of all, Luis Cordova, who has been following my steps since I first started to write about Symfony2 in 2011. He did a thorough review of the first draft. My colleagues at IPPZ have also provided me with valuable feedback, encouraging me to make some things clearer, and some things more interesting: Dennis Coorn, Matthijs van Rietschoten and Maurits Henneke. Working with them for two years, sharing concerns about maintainability, readability, reusability, and all the other -bilities, like laughability has been great fun. Thanks also to Lambert Beekhuis, organizer of the Dutch Symfony2 Usergroup meetups, for giving me some valuable feedback with regard to my English grammar.

---

[1] http://php-and-symfony.matthiasnoback.nl
[2] http://www.ippz.nl

Who should read this book

I've written this book with developers in mind who have worked with PHP for some time and with Symfony2 for a couple of weeks, maybe months. I assume you have used the official Symfony2 documentation to get acquainted with the basics of creating Symfony2 applications. I expect you to know the basic structure of an application (the standard directory structure, the way you can create or register a bundle), how you can create controllers and add routing configuration for them, how to create form types, and write Twig templates.

I also assume you have worked with some kind of persistence library, be it Doctrine ORM, Doctrine MongoDB ODM, Propel, etc. However, in the book I only refer to Doctrine libraries, to keep things simple. When you use some other library for persisting objects, you are likely able to find out how to apply some of the concepts described in this book to code written for another persistence library.

Conventions

Since this book is explicitly about Symfony2, from now on I talk about "Symfony" which looks a bit nicer.

Everything I say about Symfony is related to version 2. I've written and tested the code examples in this book with Symfony 2.3. However, they may very well also be applicable to Symfony 2.1.* and 2.2.* and maybe even to Symfony 2.0.*.

In this book I show pieces of code from Symfony itself. To make this code fit on a page and still be readable, I have sometimes modified it.

Overview of the contents

The first part of this book is called The journey from request to response. It will take you along from the first entry point of a Symfony application in the front controller to the last breath it takes before sending a response back to the client. At times I will show you how you can hook into the process and modify the flow or just change the results of the intermediate steps.

The next part is called Patterns of dependency injection. It contains a collection of patterns that are solutions to recurring problems when it comes to creating or modifying service definitions, based on a bundle's configuration. I will show you many very practical examples that you can use to model your own bundle's container extension, configuration class and compiler passes.

The third part is about Project structure. I suggest various ways to get your controllers much cleaner, by delegating actions to form handlers, domain managers and event listeners. We also take a look at state and how to avoid it in the service layer of your application.

A quick intermezzo follows then about Configuration conventions. This part should help you with setting up the configuration for your application. It encourages you and your team to settle on some kind of a configuration convention.

The fifth part is very important as it concerns every serious application, with user sessions and sensitive data. It is about Security. This would seem to be covered completely by all the Symfony components (after all the framework itself has been audited for security issues) and Twig, but unfortunately such a thing would not be possible. You always have to keep thinking about security yourself. This part of the book contains various suggestions on how to deal with security, where to keep an eye on, when you can rely on the framework and when you need to take care of things yourself.

The sixth part is about annotations. When Symfony2 was first released in 2011 it introduced annotations as a revolutionary way to configure an application from within the doc blocks of classes, methods and properties. The first chapter of this part explains how annotations work. After that, you will learn how to create your own annotations and how you can use annotations to influence the response that is generated for a request.

The final part covers all ways of Being a Symfony developer although in fact this part is one big encouragement to *not* be a Symfony developer and to write things as loosely coupled to the Symfony framework as possible. This means separating code into reusable and project-specific code, then splitting the reusable code into library and bundle code. I will discuss different other ideas that make your bundles nice, clean and friendly for other projects.

Enjoy!

I The journey from request to response

1 The `HttpKernelInterface`

Symfony is famous for its `HttpKernelInterface`:

```php
namespace Symfony\Component\HttpKernel;

use Symfony\Component\HttpFoundation\Request;
use Symfony\Component\HttpFoundation\Response;

interface HttpKernelInterface
{
    const MASTER_REQUEST = 1;
    const SUB_REQUEST = 2;

    /**
     * @return Response
     */
    public function handle(
        Request $request,
        $type = self::MASTER_REQUEST,
        $catch = true
    );
}
```

An implementation of this interface would only have to implement one method and thereby declare itself capable of converting in some way a given `Request` into a `Response`. When you take a look at any of the front controllers in the `/web` directory of a Symfony project, you can see that this `handle()` method plays a central role in processing web requests - as you might expect:

```php
// in /web/app.php
$kernel = new AppKernel('prod', false);
$request = Request::createFromGlobals();
$response = $kernel->handle($request);
$response->send();
```

First, `AppKernel` gets instantiated. This is a class specific to your project, and you can find it in `/app/AppKernel.php`. It allows you to register your bundles, and to change some major settings, like the location of the cache directory or the configuration file that should be loaded. Its constructor arguments are the name of the environment and whether or not the kernel should run in debug mode.

Environment

The environment can be any string. It is mainly a way to determine which configuration file should be loaded (e.g. `config_dev.yml` or `config_prod.yml`). This is made explicit in `AppKernel`:

```
1   public function registerContainerConfiguration(LoaderInterface $loader)
2   {
3       $loader
4           ->load(__DIR__.'/config/config_'.$this->getEnvironment().'.yml');
5   }
```

Debug mode

In debug mode you will have:

- A pretty, verbose exception page, showing all the required information for debugging problems.
- Verbose error messages in case the pretty exception page could not be rendered.
- Elaborate information about the time required to run different parts of the application (bootstrapping, database calls, template rendering, etc.).
- Extensive information about requests (using the web profiler and the accompanying toolbar).
- Automatic cache invalidation: this makes sure that changes to `config.yml`, `routing.yml` and the likes will be taken into account without recompiling the entire service container or routing matcher for each request (which would take a lot of time).

Next a `Request` object is created based on the existing PHP superglobals (`$_GET`, `$_POST`, `$_-COOKIE`, `$_FILES` and `$_SERVER`). The `Request` class together with other classes from the `HttpFoundation` component provide object-oriented ways to wrap the superglobals. These classes also cover many corner cases you may experience with different versions of PHP or on different platforms. It is wise (in a Symfony context) to always use `Request` to retrieve any data you would normally have taken directly from the superglobals.

Then the `handle()` method of the `AppKernel` instance gets called. Its only argument is the current `Request` object. The default arguments for the type of the request ("master") and whether or not to catch and handle exceptions (yes) will be added automatically.

The result of this `handle()` method is guaranteed to be an instance of `Response` (also from the `HttpFoundation` component). Finally the response will be sent back to the client that made the request - for instance a browser.

1.1 Booting the kernel

Of course, the magic happens inside the `handle()` method of the kernel. You will find this method implemented in the `Kernel` class, which is the parent class of `AppKernel`:

```
1   // in Symfony\Component\HttpKernel\Kernel
2
3   public function handle(
4       Request $request,
5       $type = HttpKernelInterface::MASTER_REQUEST,
6       $catch = true
7   ) {
8       if (false === $this->booted) {
9           $this->boot();
10      }
11
12      return $this->getHttpKernel()->handle($request, $type, $catch);
13  }
```

First of all, it is made sure that the `Kernel` is booted, before the `HttpKernel` is asked to do the rest. The process of booting includes:

- Initializing all the registered bundles
- Initializing the service container

Bundles as container extensions

Bundles are known amongst Symfony developers as the place to put your own code. Each bundle should have a name that reflects what kind of things you could do with the code inside it. For instance you may have a `BlogBundle`, a `CommunityBundle`, a `CommentBundle`, etc. You register your bundles in `AppKernel.php`, by adding them to the existing list of bundles:

```
1   class AppKernel extends Kernel
2   {
3       public function registerBundles()
4       {
5           $bundles = array(
6               new Symfony\Bundle\FrameworkBundle\FrameworkBundle(),
7               ...,
8               new Matthias\BlogBundle()
9           );
10
11          return $bundles;
12      }
13  }
```

This is definitely a good idea - it allows you to plug functionality into and out of your project with a single line of code. However, when looking at the Kernel and how it deals with all bundles, including yours, it becomes apparent that bundles are mainly treated as ways to extend the service container, not as libraries of code. This is why you find a DependencyInjection folder inside many bundles, accompanied by a {nameOfTheBundle}Extension class. During the process of initializing the service container, each bundle is allowed to register some services of its own to the service container, maybe add some parameters too, and possibly modify some service definitions before the container gets compiled and dumped to the cache directory:

```
namespace Matthias\BlogBundle\DependencyInjection;

use Symfony\Component\HttpKernel\DependencyInjection\Extension;
use Symfony\Component\Config\FileLocator;
use Symfony\Component\DependencyInjection\Loader\XmlFileLoader;

class MatthiasBlogExtension extends Extension
{
    public function load(array $configs, ContainerBuilder $container)
    {
        $loader = new XmlFileLoader($container,
            new FileLocator(__DIR__.'/../Resources/config'));

        // add service definitions to the container
        $loader->load('services.xml');

        $processedConfig = $this->processConfiguration(
            new Configuration(),
            $configs
        );

        // set a parameter
        $container->setParameter(
            'matthias_blog.comments_enabled',
            $processedConfig['enable_comments']
        );
    }

    public function getAlias()
    {
        return 'matthias_blog';
    }
}
```

The name returned by the getAlias() method of a container extension is actually the key under which you can set configuration values (for instance in config.yml):

```
1  matthias_blog:
2      enable_comments: true
```

You will read more about bundle configuration in Patterns of dependency injection.

 Every configuration key corresponds to a bundle

In the example above you saw that matthias_blog is the configuration key for settings related to the MatthiasBlogBundle. It may now not be such a big surprise that this is true for all keys you may know from config.yml and the likes: values under framework are related to the FrameworkBundle and values under security (even though they are defined in a separate file called security.yml) are related to the SecurityBundle. Simple as that!

Creating the service container

After all the bundles have been enabled to add their services and parameters, the container is finalized in a process that is called "compilation". During this process it is still possible to make some last-minute changes to service definitions or parameters. It is also the right moment to validate and optimize service definitions. Afterwards, the container is in its final form, and it gets dumped into two different formats: an XML file of all resolved definitions and parameters and a PHP file ready to be used as the one and only service container in your application.

Both files can be found in the cache directory corresponding to the environment of the kernel, for instance /app/cache/dev/appDevDebugProjectContainer.xml. The XML file looks like any regular XML service definition file, only a lot bigger:

```
1  <service id="event_dispatcher" class="...\ContainerAwareEventDispatcher">
2    <argument type="service" id="service_container"/>
3    <call method="addListenerService">
4      <argument>kernel.controller</argument>
5      ...
6    </call>
7    ...
8  </service>
```

The PHP file contains a method for each service that can be requested. Any creation logic, like controller arguments or method calls after instantiation can be found in this file, and it is therefore the perfect place to debug your service definitions in case anything appears to be wrong with them:

```
1   class appDevDebugProjectContainer extends Container
2   {
3       ...
4
5       protected function getEventDispatcherService()
6       {
7           $this->services['event_dispatcher'] =
8               $instance = new ContainerAwareEventDispatcher($this);
9
10          $instance->addListenerService('kernel.controller', ...);
11
12          ...
13
14          return $instance;
15      }
16
17      ...
18  }
```

1.2 From the `Kernel` to the `HttpKernel`

Now that the kernel is booted (i.e. all bundles are initialized, their extensions are registered, and the service container is finalized), the real handling of the request is delegated to an instance of `HttpKernel`:

```
1   // in Symfony\Component\HttpKernel\Kernel
2
3   public function handle(
4       Request $request,
5       $type = HttpKernelInterface::MASTER_REQUEST,
6       $catch = true
7   ) {
8       if (false === $this->booted) {
9           $this->boot();
10      }
11
12      return $this->getHttpKernel()->handle($request, $type, $catch);
13  }
```

The `HttpKernel` implements `HttpKernelInterface` and it truly knows how to convert a request to a response. The `handle()` method looks like this:

```
 1  public function handle(
 2      Request $request,
 3      $type = HttpKernelInterface::MASTER_REQUEST,
 4      $catch = true
 5  ) {
 6      try {
 7          return $this->handleRaw($request, $type);
 8      } catch (\Exception $e) {
 9          if (false === $catch) {
10              throw $e;
11          }
12
13          return $this->handleException($e, $request, $type);
14      }
15  }
```

As you can see, most of the work is done in the private handleRaw() method, and the try/catch block is here to capture any exceptions. When the initial argument $catch was true (which is the default value for "master" requests), every exception will be handled nicely. The HttpKernel will try to find someone who can still create a decent Response object for it (see also Exception handling).

2 Events leading to a response

The handleRaw() method of the HttpKernel is a beautiful piece of code, in which it becomes clear that handling a request is not deterministic *per se*. There are all kinds of ways in which you can hook into the process, and completely replace or just modify any intermediate result.

2.1 Early response

The first moment you can take control of handling the request, is right at the beginning. Usually the HttpKernel will try to generate a response by executing a controller. But any event listener that listens to the KernelEvents::REQUEST (kernel.request) event is allowed to generate a completely custom response:

```php
use Symfony\Component\HttpKernel\Event\GetResponseEvent;

private function handleRaw(Request $request, $type = self::MASTER_REQUEST)
{
    $event = new GetResponseEvent($this, $request, $type);
    $this->dispatcher->dispatch(KernelEvents::REQUEST, $event);

    if ($event->hasResponse()) {
        return $this->filterResponse(
            $event->getResponse(),
            $request,
            $type
        );
    }

    ...
}
```

As you can see, the event object that gets created is an instance of GetResponseEvent and it allows listeners to set a custom Response object using its setResponse() method, for example:

```
1   use Symfony\Component\HttpFoundation\Response;
2   use Symfony\Component\HttpKernel\Event\GetResponseEvent;
3
4   class MaintenanceModeListener
5   {
6       public function onKernelRequest(GetResponseEvent $event)
7       {
8           $response = new Response(
9               'This site is temporarily unavailable',
10              503
11          );
12
13          $event->setResponse($response);
14      }
15  }
```

Registering event listeners

The event dispatcher used by the HttpKernel is the one that is also available as the event_dispatcher service. When you want to automatically register some class as an event listener, you can create a service definition for it and add the tag kernel.event_listener or kernel.event_subscriber (in case you choose to implement EventSubscriberInterface).

```
1  <service id="..." class="...">
2    <tag name="kernel.event_listener"
3        event="kernel.request"
4        method="onKernelRequest" />
5  </service>
```

Or:

```
1  <service id="..." class="...">
2    <tag name="kernel.event_subscriber" />
3  </service>
```

You can optionally give your event listener a priority, so that it will take precedence over other listeners:

```
1  <service id="..." class="...">
2    <tag name="kernel.event_listener"
3        event="kernel.request"
4        method="onKernelRequest"
5        priority="100" />
6  </service>
```

The higher the number, the earlier it will be notified.

Some notable `kernel.request` event listeners

The framework itself has many listeners for the kernel.request event. These are mostly listeners to set some things straight, before letting the kernel call any controller. For instance one listener makes sure the application has a locale (either the default locale, or the _locale part from the URI), another one processes requests for fragments of pages.

There are however two main players in the early request stage: the RouterListener and the Firewall. The RouterListener takes the path info from the Request object and tries to match it to some known route. It stores the result of the matching process in the Request object as attributes, for instance the name of the controller that corresponds to the route that was matched:

```
1   namespace Symfony\Component\HttpKernel\EventListener;
2
3   class RouterListener implements EventSubscriberInterface
4   {
5       public function onKernelRequest(GetResponseEvent $event)
6       {
7           $request = $event->getRequest();
8
9           $parameters = $this->matcher->match($request->getPathInfo());
10
11          ...
12
13          $request->attributes->add($parameters);
14      }
15  }
```

When for example the matcher is asked to match /demo/hello/World, and the routing configuration looks like this:

```
1   _demo_hello:
2       path: /demo/hello/{name}
3       defaults:
4           _controller: AcmeDemoBundle:Demo:hello
```

The parameters returned by the match() call are a combination of the values defined under defaults: and the dynamic values matched by placeholders in the path (like {name}):

```
1   array(
2       '_route' => '_demo_hello',
3       '_controller' => 'AcmeDemoBundle:Demo:hello',
4       'name' => 'World'
5   );
```

These end up in the Request parameter bag called "attributes". As you would be able to guess: HttpKernel will later examine the request attributes and execute the given controller.

Another important event listener is the Firewall. As we saw above, the RouterListener does not provide the HttpKernel with a Response object, it just does some work at the beginning of a request. On the contrary, the Firewall sometimes forces a certain Response object, for instance when a user is not authenticated when he should have been, since he has requested a protected page. The Firewall (through quite a complex process) then forces a redirect to for instance a login page, or sets some headers requiring the user to enter his credentials using HTTP authentication.

2.2 Resolving the controller

We have seen above that the RouterListener sets a Request attribute called _controller, which contains some kind of reference to the controller that is to be executed. This information is not known to the HttpKernel. Instead, there is an object called ControllerResolver that is asked to return a controller for the current Request object:

```
private function handleRaw(Request $request, $type = self::MASTER_REQUEST)
{
    // "kernel.request" event

    ...

    if (false === $controller = $this->resolver->getController($request)) {
        throw new NotFoundHttpException();
    }
}
```

The resolver itself is an instance of ControllerResolverInterface:

```
namespace Symfony\Component\HttpKernel\Controller;

use Symfony\Component\HttpFoundation\Request;

interface ControllerResolverInterface
{
    public function getController(Request $request);

    public function getArguments(Request $request, $controller);
}
```

It will later be used to determine the right arguments for executing the controller. Its first task is to get the controller. The standard controller resolver takes the controller from the Request attribute _controller:

```
public function getController(Request $request)
{
    if (!$controller = $request->attributes->get('_controller')) {
        return false;
    }

    ...

    $callable = $this->createController($controller);
```

```
10
11       ...
12
13       return $callable;
14  }
```

Since in most cases the controller is a string in some kind of (short-hand) notation, the controller needs to be actually created.

 All things a controller can be

The `ControllerResolver` from the Symfony HttpKernel Component supports:

- Array callables (object/method or class/static method combinations)
- Invokable objects (objects with the magic method `__invoke()`, like anonymous functions, which are an instance of `\Closure`)
- Classes of invokable objects
- Regular functions

Any other controller that is provided as a string should be of the pattern `class::method`. However, the `ControllerResolver` defined in the `FrameworkBundle` adds some extra controller name patterns:

- `BundleName:ControllerName:actionName`
- `service_id:methodName`

After creating an instance of the controller, this specific `ControllerResolver` also checks if the controller is an instance of `ContainerAwareInterface`, and in that case it calls `setContainer()` to provide the controller with the service container. This is why the service container is already available in standard controllers.

2.3 Allow replacement of the controller

Back in the `HttpKernel` the controller is now completely available, and almost ready to be executed. But even though the controller resolver has done everything in its power to prepare a valid callable before executing it, there is a last chance to completely replace it with some other controller (which can be any callable). This chance is provided by another event: `KernelEvents::CONTROLLER` (`kernel.controller`):

```
1  use Symfony\Component\HttpKernel\Event\FilterControllerEvent;
2
3  private function handleRaw(Request $request, $type = self::MASTER_REQUEST)
4  {
5      // "kernel.request" event
6      // use the controller resolver to get the controller
7      ...
8
9      $event = new FilterControllerEvent($this, $controller, $request, $type);
10     $this->dispatcher->dispatch(KernelEvents::CONTROLLER, $event);
11     $controller = $event->getController();
12 }
```

By calling the setController() method of the FilterControllerEvent object, it is possible to override the controller that should be executed:

```
1  use Symfony\Component\HttpKernel\Event\FilterControllerEvent;
2
3  class ControllerListener
4  {
5      public function onKernelController(FilterControllerEvent $event)
6      {
7          $event->setController(...);
8      }
9  }
```

Event propagation

When you override an intermediate result, for instance when you entirely replace a controller after being notified of the kernel.filter_controller event, you may want to prevent other listeners from doing the same thing. You can do this by calling:

```
1  $event->stopPropagation();
```

Also make sure your listener has a high priority and will be called first. See also Registering event listeners.

Some notable kernel.controller listeners

The framework itself has no listeners for the kernel.controller event. There are only third-party bundles which listen to the event to anticipate the fact that the controller has been determined and that it will be executed.

The `ControllerListener` from the `SensioFrameworkExtraBundle` for instance does some very important work right before executing a controller: it collects annotations like `@Template` and `@Cache` and stores them as request attributes with the same name with an underscore as a prefix: `_template` and `_cache`. Later in the process of handling the request, these annotations (or configurations as they are called in the code of this bundle) will be used to render a template, or set some cache-related response headers.

The `ParamConverterListener` from the same bundle will convert extra controller arguments, for instance entities that should be resolved by taking the `id` value from the route:

```
/**
 * @Route("/post/{id}")
 */
public function showAction(Post $post)
{
    ...
}
```

Param converters

The `SensioFrameworkExtraBundle` ships with a `DoctrineParamConverter` which helps in converting field name/value pairs (like `id`) to an entity or a document. But you can create these "param converters" yourself too. Just implement `ParamConverterInterface`, create a service definition for it and give it a tag `request.param_converter`. See also the documentation for `@ParamConverter`[1].

2.4 Collect arguments for executing the controller

After any listener has been enabled to replace the controller, the controller we have now is the definitive one. The next step is to collect the arguments that should be used when executing it:

```
private function handleRaw(Request $request, $type = self::MASTER_REQUEST)
{
    // "kernel.request" event
    // use the controller resolver to get the controller
    // "kernel.controller" event
    ...

    $arguments = $this->resolver->getArguments($request, $controller);
}
```

---

[1]http://symfony.com/doc/current/bundles/SensioFrameworkExtraBundle/annotations/converters.html

The controller resolver is asked to supply the controller arguments. The standard `ControllerResolver` from the HttpKernel Component uses reflection and the attributes from the `Request` object to resolve the controller arguments. It loops over all the parameters from the controller method. The following logic is used to determine each argument:

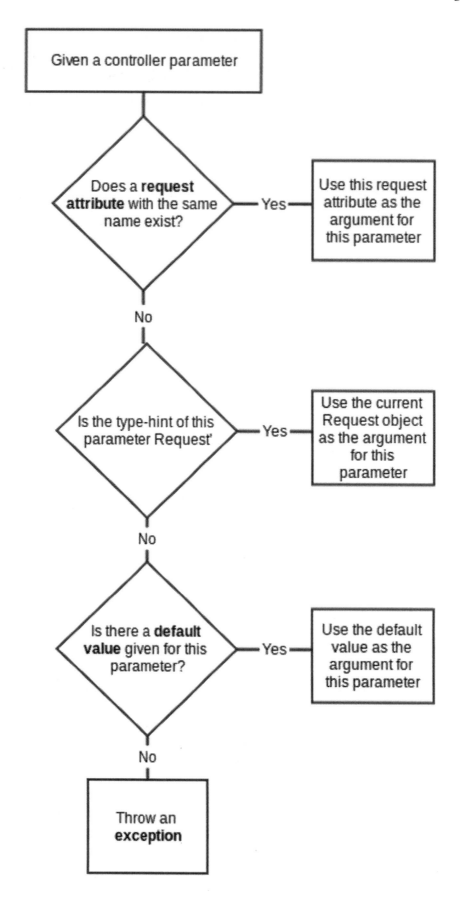

Resolving a controller argument

2.5 Execute the controller

Finally, it's time to execute the controller. The response is caught and further processed.

```
1  private function handleRaw(Request $request, $type = self::MASTER_REQUEST)
2  {
3      // "kernel.request" event
4      // use the controller resolver to get the controller
5      // "kernel.controller" event
6      // use the controller resolver to get the controller arguments
7      ...
8
9      $response = call_user_func_array($controller, $arguments);
10
11     if (!$response instanceof Response) {
12         ...
13     }
14 }
```

As you may remember from the Symfony documentation, a controller should return a Response object. If it doesn't, some other part of the application should be able to convert the return value to a Response object in some way or another.

2.6 Enter the view layer

When you choose to return a Response object directly from your controller, you can thereby effectively by-pass the templating engine:

```
1  class SomeController
2  {
3      public function simpleAction()
4      {
5          return new Response(
6              '<html><body><p>Pure old-fashioned HTML</p></body></html>'
7          );
8      }
9  }
```

However, when you return anything else (though usually an array of template variables), this return value needs to be converted to a Response object before it can be used as a decent response to be sent back to the client. The HttpKernel is explicitly not coupled to a specific templating engine like Twig. Instead it uses the event dispatcher again to allow any listener to the KernelEvents::VIEW event (kernel.view) to set a proper response based on the return value of the controller (though it may choose to ignore this value entirely):

```
1   use Symfony\Component\HttpKernel\Event\GetResponseForControllerResultEvent;
2
3   private function handleRaw(Request $request, $type = self::MASTER_REQUEST)
4   {
5       // "kernel.request" event
6       // use the controller resolver to get the controller
7       // "kernel.controller" event
8       // use the controller resolver to get the controller arguments
9       // execute the controller
10      ...
11
12      $event = new GetResponseForControllerResultEvent(
13          $this,
14          $request,
15          $type,
16          $response
17      );
18      $this->dispatcher->dispatch(KernelEvents::VIEW, $event);
19
20      if ($event->hasResponse()) {
21          $response = $event->getResponse();
22      }
23
24      if (!$response instanceof Response) {
25          // the kernel REALLY needs a response by now
26
27          throw new \LogicException(...);
28      }
29  }
```

Listeners to this event can call setResponse() on the GetResponseForControllerResultEvent
object:

```
1   use Symfony\Component\HttpKernel\Event\GetResponseForControllerResultEvent;
2
3   class ViewListener
4   {
5       public function onKernelView(GetResponseForControllerResultEvent $event)
6       {
7           $response = new Response(...);
8
9           $event->setResponse($response);
10      }
11  }
```

A notable `kernel.view` listener

The `TemplateListener` from the `SensioFrameworkExtraBundle` takes the controller result and uses it as template variables to render the template that was specified using the `@Template` annotation (which was stored as the request attribute `_template`):

```
public function onKernelView(GetResponseForControllerResultEvent $event)
{
    $parameters = $event->getControllerResult();

    // get the templating engine
    $templating = ...;

    $event->setResponse(
        $templating->renderResponse($template, $parameters)
    );
}
```

2.7 Filter the response

In the end, right before returning the Response object as the final result of handling the given Request object, any listener for the `KernelEvents::RESPONSE` event (`kernel.response`) will be notified:

```
private function handleRaw(Request $request, $type = self::MASTER_REQUEST)
{
    // "kernel.request" event
    // use the controller resolver to get the controller
    // "kernel.controller" event
    // use the controller resolver to get the controller arguments
    // convert the controller result to a Response object

    return $this->filterResponse($response, $request, $type);
}


private function filterResponse(Response $response, Request $request, $type)
{
    $event = new FilterResponseEvent($this, $request, $type, $response);

    $this->dispatcher->dispatch(KernelEvents::RESPONSE, $event);

    return $event->getResponse();
}
```

Event listeners are allowed to modify the Response object and even to replace it completely:

```
 1  class ResponseListener
 2  {
 3      public function onKernelResponse(FilterResponseEvent $event)
 4      {
 5          $response = $event->getResponse();
 6
 7          $response->headers->set('X-Framework', 'Symfony2');
 8
 9          // or
10
11          $event->setResponse(new Response(...));
12      }
13  }
```

Notable `kernel.response` listeners

The `WebDebugToolbarListener` from the `WebProfilerBundle` injects some HTML and JavaScript code at the end of the response to make sure the profiler toolbar appears (usually at the bottom of the page).

The `ContextListener` from the Symfony Security Component stores a serialized version of the current security token in the session. This allows for a much faster authentication process during the next request. The Security Component also has a `ResponseListener` that sets a cookie containing "remember-me" information. Its contents can be used to auto-login a user even when his original session was already destroyed.

3 Exception handling

It is not unlikely that during the long journey from request to response some kind of an error or exception occurs. By default, the kernel is instructed to catch any exception and even then it tries to find an appropriate response for it. As we already saw, the entire request handling gets wrapped in a try/catch block:

```php
public function handle(
    Request $request,
    $type = HttpKernelInterface::MASTER_REQUEST,
    $catch = true
) {
    try {
        return $this->handleRaw($request, $type);
    } catch (\Exception $e) {
        if (false === $catch) {
            throw $e;
        }

        return $this->handleException($e, $request, $type);
    }
}
```

When $catch equals true, the handleException() method is called and is expected to create a response. This method dispatches a KernelEvents::EXCEPTION event (kernel.exception) with a GetResponseForExceptionEvent object.

```php
use Symfony\Component\HttpKernel\Event\GetResponseForExceptionEvent;

private function handleException(\Exception $e, $request, $type)
{
    $event = new GetResponseForExceptionEvent($this, $request, $type, $e);
    $this->dispatcher->dispatch(KernelEvents::EXCEPTION, $event);

    // a listener might have replaced the exception
    $e = $event->getException();

    if (!$event->hasResponse()) {
        throw $e;
    }
```

```
14
15    $response = $event->getResponse();
16
17        ...
18  }
```

Listeners for the kernel.exception event are allowed to:

- Set a proper Response object for this specific exception.
- Replace the original Exception object.

When none of the listeners has called setResponse() on the event object, the exception will be thrown (again), but this time it will not be handled automatically. So in case your display_errors PHP setting equals true, PHP just renders it as-is.

In case any of the listeners has set a Response object, the HttpKernel examines this object in order to set the right status code for the response:

```
1   // the developer asked for a specific status code
2   if ($response->headers->has('X-Status-Code')) {
3       $response->setStatusCode($response->headers->get('X-Status-Code'));
4
5       $response->headers->remove('X-Status-Code');
6   } elseif (
7       !$response->isClientError()
8       && !$response->isServerError()
9       && !$response->isRedirect()
10  ) {
11      // ensure that we actually have an error response
12      if ($e instanceof HttpExceptionInterface) {
13          // keep the HTTP status code and headers
14          $response->setStatusCode($e->getStatusCode());
15          $response->headers->add($e->getHeaders());
16      } else {
17          $response->setStatusCode(500);
18      }
19  }
```

This is quite useful: we can enforce a certain status code to be used by adding an X-Status-Code header to the Response object (remember: this only works for exceptions that are caught by the HttpKernel), or by throwing exceptions that implement HttpExceptionInterface. Otherwise the status code defaults to 500 - Internal server error. This is much better than the standard PHP behavior, which will return a response with status 200 - OK, when an error has occurred.

When an event listener has set a Response object, this response is not handled any differently than a normal response, so the last step in handling an exception is to filter the response. When another exception gets thrown while filtering the response, this exception will simply be ignored, and the unfiltered response will be sent to the client.

```
1  try {
2      return $this->filterResponse($response, $request, $type);
3  } catch (\Exception $e) {
4      return $response;
5  }
```

3.1 Notable `kernel.exception` listeners

The ExceptionListener from the HttpKernel Component itself tries to handle an exception by logging it (when a logger is available) and by executing a controller which may render a page with some information about the error. Usually this is the controller defined in `config.yml`:

```
1  twig:
2      # points to Symfony\Bundle\TwigBundle\Controller\ExceptionController
3      exception_controller: twig.controller.exception:showAction
```

Another important listener is the ExceptionListener from the Security Component. This listener checks if the original exception that was thrown is an instance of AuthenticationException or AccessDeniedException. In the first case, it starts the authentication process if this is possible. In the second case, it tries to re-authenticate the user or lets the access denied handler deal with the situation.

4 Sub-requests

Maybe you noticed the `$type` argument of the `HttpKernel::handle()` method:

```
1  public function handle(
2      Request $request,
3      $type = HttpKernelInterface::MASTER_REQUEST,
4      $catch = true
5  ) {
6      ...
7  }
```

There are two request types defined as constants in `HttpKernelInterface`:

1. `HttpKernelInterface::MASTER_REQUEST`, the master request
2. `HttpKernelInterface::SUB_REQUEST`, a sub-request

For each request to your PHP application, the first request that is handled by the kernel is of the first type, `HttpKernelInterface::MASTER_REQUEST`. This is rather implicit, since it is caused by leaving the `$type` argument away in the front controller (`app.php` or `app_dev.php`):

```
1  $response = $kernel->handle($request);
```

Many event listeners listen to the kernel events as discussed above, but only act when the request is of type `HttpKernelInterface::MASTER_REQUEST`. For instance, the `Firewall` does not do anything if the request is a sub-request:

```
1  public function onKernelRequest(GetResponseEvent $event)
2  {
3      if (HttpKernelInterface::MASTER_REQUEST !== $event->getRequestType()) {
4          return;
5      }
6
7      ...
8  }
```

4.1 When are sub-requests used?

Sub-requests are used to isolate the creation of a `Response` object. For example, when an exception is caught by the kernel, the standard exception handler tries to execute a designated exception controller (see above). To do this, a sub-request is created:

```
1  public function onKernelException(GetResponseForExceptionEvent $event)
2  {
3      $request = $event->getRequest();
4
5      ...
6
7      $request = $request->duplicate(null, null, $attributes);
8      $request->setMethod('GET');
9
10     $response = $event
11         ->getKernel()
12         ->handle($request, HttpKernelInterface::SUB_REQUEST, true);
13
14     $event->setResponse($response);
15 }
```

Also, whenever you render another controller as part of a Twig template, a sub-request is created and handled:

```
1  {{ render(controller('BlogBundle:Post:list')) }}
```

 When writing your own kernel event listener...

Ask yourself if the event listener should react to master requests, sub-requests or both. Use a guard clause to return early (see the example above).

II Patterns of dependency injection

5 What is a bundle?

As we saw in the previous chapter: running a Symfony application means booting the kernel and handling a request or executing a command, where booting the kernel means: loading all bundles and registering their service container extensions (which can be found in the DependencyInjection folder of a bundle). The container extension usually loads a services.xml file (but this can be anything) and the bundle's configuration, defined in a separate class, usually in the same namespace, called Configuration. These things together (*bundle, container extension* and *configuration*) can be used to wire up your bundle: you can define parameters and services so that the functionality you provide inside your bundle is available to other parts of the application. You can even go one step further and register *compiler passes* to further modify the service container before it gets its final form.

After creating many bundles, I concluded that much of my work as a developer which is specific for a Symfony application consists of writing code for exactly these things: bundle, extension and configuration classes and compiler passes. When you know how to write good code, you still need to know how to create good bundles, and this basically means that you need to know how to create good service definitions. There are many ways to do this, and in this chapter I will describe most of them. Knowing your options enables you to make better choices when looking for a dependency injection pattern.

 Don't use generation commands

When you start using Symfony, you may be tempted to use commands provided by the SensioGeneratorBundle to generate bundles, controllers, entities and form types. I do not recommend this. These generated classes can be nice to keep as a reference for creating these classes manually, but in general they contain too much code you don't need, or that you don't need to begin with. So use these generate commands once, take a look how things should be done, and then learn yourself to do things like that, instead of relying on these commands. It will really make you a faster developer, who understands the framework well.

6 Service patterns

A service is an object, registered at the service container under a certain id. A service definition is a bit of configuration to define such a service, so that it can be instantiated at any time by the service container.

6.1 Required dependencies

Most objects need some other objects and maybe a scalar value (like an API key) or an array of values (either scalar values or objects) to be able to do their work. These are called its dependencies. We will first discuss how you can define required dependencies for services.

Required constructor arguments

The usual way to make sure a service gets its dependencies is by injecting them as constructor arguments:

```
1  class TokenProvider
2  {
3      private $storage;
4
5      public function __construct(TokenStorageInterface $storage)
6      {
7          $this->storage = $storage;
8      }
9  }
```

The service definition for the `TokenProvider` class would look like this:

```
1  <service id="token_provider" class="TokenProvider">
2    <argument type="service" id="token_storage" />
3  </service>
4
5  <service id="token_storage" class="...">
6  </service>
```

The first argument of the `token_provider` service is a reference to the `token_storage` service. The class used for the storage should therefore implement `TokenStorageInterface`, or else it is not a correct argument and you get a `Fatal error`.

Abstract definitions for extra arguments

Say you have another token provider, an `ExpiringTokenProvider`, which extends from `TokenProvider`, but has an extra constructor argument, `$lifetime`:

```
 1  class ExpiringTokenProvider extends TokenProvider
 2  {
 3      private $lifetime;
 4
 5      public function __construct(TokenStorageInterface $storage, $lifetime)
 6      {
 7          $this->lifetime = $lifetime;
 8
 9          parent::__construct($storage);
10      }
11  }
```

When creating a service definition for this second token provider, you could just copy the argument from the existing token_provider definition:

```
 1  <service id="expiring_token_provider" class="ExpiringTokenProvider">
 2    <argument type="service" id="token_storage" />
 3    <argument>3600</argument><!-- lifetime -->
 4  </service>
```

In these situations it's better to create a parent service definition, which you can use to define everything that its child definitions should have in common:

```
 1  <service id="abstract_token_provider" abstract="true">
 2    <argument type="service" id="token_storage" />
 3  </service>
 4
 5  <service id="token_provider" class="TokenProvider"
 6    parent="abstract_token_provider">
 7  </service>
 8
 9  <service id="expiring_token_provider" class="ExpiringTokenProvider"
10    parent="abstract_token_provider">
11    <argument>3600</argument><!-- lifetime -->
12  </service>
```

The abstract service has one argument and is marked as abstract. The token provider services mention abstract_token_provider as their parent. The token_provider service has no extra arguments, so it just inherits the first constructor argument from abstract_token_provider. The expiring_token_provider service also inherits the token_storage service as the first argument, but adds an extra argument for $lifetime.

Inherited properties

Whether or not the parent of a service is abstract, these are the properties a child service definition inherits from its parent definition:

- Class
- Constructor arguments (in order of appearance)
- Method calls made to it after creation
- Property injections[*]
- Factory class or factory service, and factory method
- Configurator (a bit exotic, not discussed here)
- File (required for creating this service)
- Whether or not the service is public

[*] All the disadvantages of property injection are listed here[1]

Required setter calls

In some cases you don't want to override the constructor and add extra required arguments, or some of the dependencies are not yet determined at the time the service gets created. For these situations, you may add setter methods to your class, to allow someone to inject a dependency immediately after the service was created (or in fact, at any moment afterwards):

```
1   class SomeController
2   {
3       private $container;
4
5       public function setContainer(ContainerInterface $container)
6       {
7           $this->container = $container;
8       }
9
10      public function indexAction()
11      {
12          $service = $this->container->get('...');
13      }
14  }
```

Since (as you can see in the example above) an instance of ContainerInterface really is required to run the indexAction() method, this is a *required* setter call. So in your service definition you should take care that the service container gets injected:

---

[1]http://symfony.com/doc/current/components/dependency_injection/types.html#property-injection

```
1  <service id="some_controller" class="SomeController">
2    <call method="setContainer">
3      <argument type="service" id="service_container" />
4    </call>
5  </service>
```

The advantage of using setters for dependency injection is that you are not required to have a constructor argument for the dependency anymore. Sometimes this means that you don't need to have a constructor at all, or that you can leave an existing constructor as it is. The disadvantage is that you may forget to call the setter, so that one of the dependencies of an object is missing. In the example above, a call will then be made to the get() method of a non-object (null) which results in PHP throwing a Fatal error. In my opinion, this one disadvantage, is usually much bigger than any advantage you can think of, since it introduces a code smell called "temporal coupling". It thereby makes your class somewhat unreliable.

To prevent these severe crashes from happening (and to help a developer who encounters the error to fix the problem) you may choose to wrap calls to dependencies that should have been injected using a setter:

```
1  class SomeController
2  {
3      public function indexAction()
4      {
5          $service = $this->getContainer()->get('...');
6      }
7
8      private function getContainer()
9      {
10         if (!($this->container instanceof ContainerInterface)) {
11             throw new \RuntimeException('Service container is missing');
12         }
13
14         return $this->container;
15     }
16 }
```

 ContainerAware

The Symfony DependencyInjection Component contains a ContainerAwareInterface and an abstract ContainerAware class which you can use to indicate that a class is "aware" of the service container. This will give you a setter called setContainer(), by which you can provide the service container from the outside. Controllers that implement ContainerAwareInterface, automatically receive the container via this setter. The standard Controller from the Symfony FrameworkBundle is container-aware. See also Resolving the controller

Method calls in abstract definitions

When you create container-aware services, you will have much code duplication in your service definitions. It may then be a good idea to add the call to `setContainer()` to an abstract service definition:

```
1  <service id="abstract_container_aware" abstract="true">
2    <call method="setContainer">
3      <argument type="service" id="service_container" />
4    </call>
5  </service>
6
7  <service id="some_controller" class="SomeController"
8    parent="abstract_container_aware">
9  </service>
```

Naming parent service definitions

Parent service definitions don't need to be abstract definitions. However, when you leave out the `abstract="true"` attribute, the parent definition will be treated like a normal service definition (and also validated like one).

When you have an abstract service definition, mark it as abstract by setting the `abstract` attribute to `true` *and* by adding `abstract_` in front of its service id (just like abstract classes by convention start with `Abstract`).

When you have a parent service definition, which should also be treated as a service by itself, don't add an `abstract` attribute and maybe add `base_` in front of its service id.

6.2 Optional dependencies

Sometimes dependencies are optional. When you think about the term "optional dependencies" this feels a bit like a contradiction, because if you don't *really* depend on them, they are not dependencies. However, there are situations where a service knows how to use another service, but does not actually *need* it for doing its job. For instance, a service may know how to deal with a logger to log some things for debugging purposes.

Optional constructor arguments

In case your service's class knows how to work with a logger, it may have an optional constructor argument for it:

```
1   use Symfony\Component\EventDispatcher\EventDispatcherInterface;
2   use Psr\Log\LoggerInterface;
3
4   class AuthenticationListener
5   {
6       private $eventDispatcher;
7       private $logger;
8
9       public function __construct(
10          EventDispatcherInterface $eventDispatcher,
11          LoggerInterface $logger = null
12      ) {
13          $this->eventDispatcher = $eventDispatcher;
14          $this->logger = $logger;
15      }
16  }
```

For constructor arguments that should be either an object of the given class/interface, or nothing, you can use the default value null. Then in your service definition, choose a strategy for dealing with a missing service:

```
1   <service id="authentication_listener" class="AuthenticationListener">
2     <argument type="service" id="logger" on-invalid="ignore" />
3   </service>
```

The ignore strategy is currently equivalent to the null strategy, in that it will call the constructor with a null value instead of the requested service. There is also the exception strategy, which is the default strategy. This will raise an exception when the injected service could not be found.

Checking for optionally injected dependencies

When you want to check whether or not an optional dependency was injected, you should do it like this:

```
1   if ($this->logger instanceof LoggerInterface) {
2       ...
3   }
```

This is much more reliable than using:

```
1   if ($this->logger !== null) {
2       ...
3   }
```

Think about it: if something is not the same as null, can it then be inferred that it is a logger?

Optional setter calls

Just like with required dependencies, there is sometimes a good case for injecting optional dependencies using a setter. Especially when you don't want to muddle with the constructor signature:

```
1   class AuthenticationListener
2   {
3       private $eventDispatcher;
4       private $logger;
5
6       public function __construct(EventDispatcherInterface $eventDispatcher)
7       {
8           $this->eventDispatcher = $eventDispatcher;
9       }
10
11      public function setLogger(LoggerInterface $logger = null)
12      {
13          $this->logger = $logger;
14      }
15  }
```

In the service definition you can add a call to setLogger() with the logger service as an argument. When this service does not exist, you can indicate that it should be ignored (so that this dependency is truly optional):

```
1  <service id="authentication_listener" class="AuthenticationListener">
2    <call method="setLogger">
3      <argument type="service" id="logger" on-invalid="ignore" />
4    </call>
5  </service>
```

The argument of the call to setLogger() can be null (when the service is not defined), but the method will be called anyway, so you have to take good care that null is in fact an acceptable argument of the setLogger() method.

 Mark dependencies as non-public

When you program in a nice object-oriented style, you always end up with lots of small services, each with just one responsibility. Higher-level services will have them injected as dependencies. The lower-level services are not meant to be used on their own; they only make sense as collaborators of high-level services. In order to prevent other parts of the system to retrieve low-level services from the service container directly:

```
1  $container->get('low_level_service_id');
```

You should mark these services as non-public:

```
1  <service id="low_level_service_id" class="..." public="false">
2  </service>
```

6.3 A collection of services

In most situations you inject specific services as constructor or setter arguments. But sometimes you need to inject a collection of services, that are treated in the same way, for instance when you want to provide several alternative ways (strategies) to achieve something:

```
1  class ObjectRenderer
2  {
3      private $renderers;
4
5      public function __construct(array $renderers)
6      {
7          $this->renderers = $renderers;
8      }
9
10     public function render($object)
```

```
11      {
12          foreach ($this->renderers as $renderer) {
13              if ($renderer->supports($object) {
14                  return $renderer->render($object);
15              }
16          }
17      }
18  }
```

In a service definition this may look like:

```
1  <service id="object_renderer" class="ObjectRenderer">
2    <argument type="collection">
3      <argument type="service" id="domain_object_renderer" />
4      <argument type="service" id="user_renderer" />
5    </argument>
6  </service>
```

This `collection` type argument will be converted to an array, containing the services referenced by their ids:

```
1  array(
2      0 => ...
3      1 => ...
4  )
```

Optionally you could also give each argument inside the collection a `key` attribute.

```
1  <service id="object_renderer" class="ObjectRenderer">
2    <argument type="collection">
3      <argument
4        key="domain_object" type="service"
5        id="domain_object_renderer" />
6      <argument
7        key="user" type="service"
8        id="user_renderer" />
9    </argument>
10 </service>
```

The value of the `key` attribute will be used as the key for each value of the collection:

```
1  array(
2      'domain_object' => ...
3      'user' => ...
4  )
```

Multiple method calls

When you read the code of the ObjectRenderer class again in "strict" mode, it appears you cannot trust the $renderers array to contain only valid renderers (which, let's say, implement RendererInterface). Therefore, you may decide to dedicate a special method for adding a renderer:

```
1  class ObjectRenderer
2  {
3      private $renderers;
4
5      public function __construct()
6      {
7          $this->renderers = array();
8      }
9
10     public function addRenderer($name, RendererInterface $renderer)
11     {
12         $this->renderers[$name] = $renderer;
13     }
14 }
```

Of course, when the name is irrelevant, leave out the $name parameter. What matters is: whenever anybody calls the addRenderer method and provides an object which is not an implementation of RendererInterface, he will not succeed, because of the type-hint mismatch.

The service definition should now be changed to call the addRenderer() method for each of the available renderers:

```
1  <service id="object_renderer" class="ObjectRenderer">
2    <call method="addRenderer">
3      <argument>domain_object</argument>
4      <argument type="service" id="domain_object_renderer" />
5    </call>
6    <call method="addRenderer">
7      <argument>user</argument>
8      <argument type="service" id="user_renderer" />
9    </argument>
10 </service>
```

The best of both worlds

It may be better to combine the two options above, allowing developers to provide both an initial collection of renderers through a constructor argument and/or to add renderers one by one using the addRenderer() method:

```
1  class ObjectRenderer
2  {
3      private $renderers;
4
5      public function __construct(array $renderers)
6      {
7          foreach ($renderers as $name => $renderer) {
8              $this->addRenderer($name, $renderer);
9          }
10     }
11
12     public function addRenderer($name, RendererInterface $renderer)
13     {
14         $this->renderers[$name] = $renderer;
15     }
16 }
```

Service tags

We already have a nice setup for manually adding renderers, but what if other parts of your application (like other bundles) should be able to register specific renderers? The best way to do this is by using service tags:

```
1  <!-- in some other bundle -->
2  <service id="date_time_renderer" class="DateTimeRenderer">
3    <tag name="specific_renderer" alias="date_time" />
4  </service>
```

Each tag has a name, which you can choose yourself. Each tag can also have any number of extra attributes (like alias above). These attributes allow you to further specify any requested behavior.

To collect services with these tags, you have to create a compiler pass like this one:

```php
1   namespace Matthias\RendererBundle\DependencyInjection\Compiler;
2
3   use Symfony\Component\DependencyInjection\Compiler\CompilerPassInterface;
4   use Symfony\Component\DependencyInjection\ContainerBuilder;
5   use Symfony\Component\DependencyInjection\Reference;
6
7   class RenderersPass implements CompilerPassInterface
8   {
9       public function process(ContainerBuilder $container)
10      {
11          // collect all tagged services in the entire project
12          $taggedServiceIds
13              = $container ->findTaggedServiceIds('specific_renderer');
14
15          $objectRendererDefinition
16              = $container->getDefinition('object_renderer');
17
18          foreach ($taggedServiceIds as $serviceId => $tags) {
19
20              // services can have many tag elements with the same tag name
21              foreach ($tags as $tagAttributes) {
22
23                  // call addRenderer() to register this specific renderer
24                  $objectRendererDefinition
25                      ->addMethodCall('addRenderer', array(
26                          $tagAttributes['alias'],
27                          new Reference($serviceId),
28                      ));
29              }
30          }
31      }
32  }
```

Register this compiler pass in your bundle class:

```
1  use Matthias\RendererBundle\DependencyInjection\Compiler\RenderersPass;
2  use Symfony\Component\DependencyInjection\ContainerBuilder;
3
4  class RendererBundle extends Bundle
5  {
6      public function build(ContainerBuilder $container)
7      {
8          $container->addCompilerPass(new RenderersPass());
9      }
10 }
```

Inside the process() method of the compiler pass, first all tags with the name specific_-renderer are collected. This will result in an array of which the keys are service ids and the values are arrays of attribute arrays. This is because each service definition can have multiple tags with the same name (but maybe with different attributes).

Then, the service definition for the ObjectRenderer class is retrieved and while iterating over the tags, a Reference is created which refers to each renderer service that is tagged as "specific_renderer" and together with the provided value for alias, these are used as arguments to a call to the method addRenderer().

All of this means that when the object_renderer service is requested, first of all an instance of ObjectRenderer gets created. But afterwards, some calls are made to its addRenderer() method to add the specific renderers tagged as specific_renderer.

Single method call

There are many possible approaches when collecting services in a compiler pass. For instance, you can collect service references in an array and set them all at once, by adding a method call to setRenderers():

```
1  class RenderersPass implements CompilerPassInterface
2  {
3      public function process(ContainerBuilder $container)
4      {
5          $taggedServiceIds = ...;
6
7          $objectRendererDefinition = ...;
8
9          $renderers = array();
10
11         foreach ($taggedServiceIds as $serviceId => $tags) {
12             foreach ($tags as $tagAttributes) {
13                 $name = $tagAttributes['alias'];
14                 $renderer = new Reference($serviceId);
```

```
15                    $renderers[$name] = $renderer;
16                }
17            }
18
19        $objectRendererDefinition
20            ->addMethodCall('setRenderers', array($renderers));
21        }
22 }
```

Replacing a single argument

When it's possible - like in one of the examples above - to inject a collection of renderers as a constructor argument, there is another way you can do this: set a constructor argument directly:

```
1  class RenderersPass implements CompilerPassInterface
2  {
3      public function process(ContainerBuilder $container)
4      {
5          $taggedServiceIds = ...;
6
7          $objectRendererDefinition = ...;
8
9          $renderers = array();
10
11         // collect service references
12         ...
13
14         $objectRendererDefinition->replaceArgument(0, $renderers);
15     }
16 }
```

Replacing arguments can only be done when you have defined them in the first place (for instance as an empty argument):

```
1  <service id="object_renderer" class="ObjectRenderer">
2    <argument /><!-- specific renderers -->
3  </service>
```

Service ids instead of references

Whenever you request the object_renderer service, all the specific renderers are instantiated too. Depending on the cost of instantiating these renderers it could be a good idea to add support for lazy-loading. This can be accomplished by making the ObjectRenderer container-aware and by injecting service ids, not the services themselves:

```
1    class LazyLoadingObjectRenderer
2    {
3        private $container;
4        private $renderers;
5
6        public function __construct(ContainerInterface $container)
7        {
8            $this->container = $container;
9        }
10
11       public function addRenderer($name, $renderer)
12       {
13           $this->renderers[$name] = $renderer;
14       }
15
16       public function render($object)
17       {
18           foreach ($this->renderers as $name => $renderer) {
19               if (is_string($renderer)) {
20                   // $renderer is assumed to be a service id
21                   $renderer = $this->container->get($renderer);
22               }
23
24               // check if the renderer is an instance of RendererInterface
25               ...
26           }
27       }
28   }
```

The compiler pass should be modified to not pass references to services, but just service ids:

```
1    class RenderersPass implements CompilerPassInterface
2    {
3        public function process(ContainerBuilder $container)
4        {
5            $taggedServiceIds = ...;
6
7            $objectRendererDefinition = ...;
8
9            foreach ($taggedServiceIds as $serviceId => $tags) {
10               foreach ($tags as $tagAttributes) {
11                   $objectRendererDefinition
12                       ->addMethodCall('addRenderer', array(
```

```
13                        $tagAttributes['alias'],
14                        $serviceId,
15                    ));
16                }
17            }
18        }
19 }
```

Also don't forget to provide the service container as a constructor argument:

```
1 <service id="object_renderer" class="LazyLoadingObjectRenderer">
2   <argument type="service" id="service_container" />
3 </service>
```

Of course, any of the strategies mentioned above can be used with this lazy-loading class (single method call, multiple method calls or argument replacement).

Before you consider changing your class to make use of the service container directly, please read the chapter Reduce coupling to the framework, specifically The performance issue.

6.4 Delegated creation

Instead of fully defining services upfront by a service definition with a class, arguments and method calls, you can also leave the details to be figured out at runtime, by delegating the creation of services to a factory method. Factory methods can be either static methods or object methods. In the first case, you can provide the class name and the method name as attributes of the service definition:

```
1 <service id="some_service" class="ClassOfResultingObject"
2   factory-class="Some\Factory" factory-method="create">
3   <argument>...</argument>
4 </service>
```

When some_service is being requested for the first time, the service will be retrieved by calling Some\Factory::create() statically with any arguments provided. The result will be stored in memory, so the factory method is called only once.

Most factory methods nowadays are not static anymore, which means that the factory method should be called on an instance of the factory itself. This instance should be defined as a service:

```
1   <!-- a service created by some_factory_service -->
2   <service id="some_service" class="ClassOfResultingObject"
3     factory-service="some_factory_service" factory-method="create">
4     <argument>...</argument>
5   </service>
6
7   <!-- the factory -->
8   <service id="some_factory_service" class="Some\Factory">
9   </service>
```

Not so useful

Though the options for delegating the creation of services to other services seem really great, I have not used them very often. They are almost exclusively useful when you are creating service definitions for older PHP classes since in the (not so distant) past, creation logic was often hidden inside static factory classes (remember `Doctrine_Core::getTable()`?).

My objection to factory classes with static factory methods is that static code is global code and that executing that code may have side effects that can not be isolated (for instance in a test scenario). Besides, any dependency of such a static factory method has to be by definition static itself, which is also really bad for isolation and prevents you from replacing (part of) the creation logic by your own code.

Factory objects (or factory services) are slightly better. However, the need for them very likely points to some kind of design problem. A service should not need a factory, since it will be created only once in a predetermined (and deterministic) way and from then on be perfectly reusable by any other object. The only things that are dynamic about a service, should be the arguments of the methods that are part of its public interface (see also State and context).

Sometimes useful

One particularly nice example of using a factory service and method for retrieving a service is the case of a Doctrine repository. When you need one, you would normally inject an entity manager as a constructor argument and later retrieve a specific repository:

```php
1   use Doctrine\ORM\EntityManager;
2
3   class SomeClass
4   {
5       public function __construct(EntityManager $entityManager)
6       {
7           $this->entityManager = $entityManager;
8       }
9
10      public function doSomething()
```

```
11      {
12          $repository = $this->entityManager->getRepository('User');
13
14          ...
15      }
16  }
```

But using a factory service and method you could directly inject the correct repository itself:

```
1  class SomeClass
2  {
3      public function __construct(UserRepository $userRepository)
4      {
5          $this->userRepository = $userRepository;
6      }
7  }
```

This is the corresponding service definition:

```
1  <service id="some_service" class="SomeClass">
2      <argument type="user_repository" />
3  </service>
4
5  <service id="user_repository" class="UserRepository"
6      factory-service="entity_manager" factory-method="getRepository">
7      <argument>User</argument>
8  </service>
```

By looking at the constructor arguments of SomeClass it is immediately clear that it needs a User repository, which is much more specific and communicative than the earlier example in which SomeClass needed an EntityManager. Besides making the class itself much cleaner, it will also make it much easier to create a stand-in object for the repository when you are writing a unit test for this class. Instead of creating a mock for both the entity manager and the repository, you only have to create one for the repository itself.

6.5 Manually creating services

Usually you create services by loading service definitions from a file:

```
1  use Symfony\Component\HttpKernel\DependencyInjection\Extension;
2  use Symfony\Component\Config\FileLocator;
3  use Symfony\Component\DependencyInjection\Loader\XmlFileLoader;
4
5  class SomeBundleExtension extends Extension
6  {
7      public function load(array $configs, ContainerBuilder $container)
8      {
9          $locator = new FileLocator(__DIR__.'/../Resources/config');
10         $loader = new XmlFileLoader($container, $locator);
11         $loader->load('services.xml');
12     }
13 }
```

But some services can not be defined in a configuration file. They should be defined dynamically, because their name, class, arguments, tags, etc. are not fixed.

Definition

Manually creating a service definition means creating an instance of Definition, and optionally providing a class name. The definition will get its identifier when it is set on the ContainerBuilder instance:

```
1  use Symfony\Component\DependencyInjection\Definition;
2
3  $class = ...; // set a class name for the definition
4
5  $definition = new Definition($class);
6
7  $container->setDefinition('the_service_id', $definition);
```

The equivalent of this in XML would be:

```
1  <service id="the_service_id" class="...">
2  </service>
```

You can make the definition non-public if it only exists as a dependency of other services:

```
1  $definition->setPublic(false);
```

Arguments

When the service requires some constructor arguments, you may set them all at once:

```
 1   use Symfony\Component\DependencyInjection\Reference;
 2
 3   $definition->setArguments(array(
 4       new Reference('logger') // reference to another service
 5       true // boolean argument,
 6       array(
 7           'table_name' => 'users'
 8       ) // array argument
 9       ...
10   );
```

Arguments should be either references to other services, array values or scalar values (or a mix of these). This is because all service definitions will eventually be stored as a simple PHP file. A reference to another service can be created by using a Reference object with the id of the service that should be injected.

You can also add the arguments one by one, in the right order:

```
 1   $definition->addArgument(new Reference('logger'));
 2   $definition->addArgument(true);
 3   ...
```

Finally, when you are modifying an existing service definition with a list of arguments, you could replace them by providing their numeric index:

```
 1   $definition->setArguments(array(null, null));
 2
 3   ...
 4
 5   $definition->replaceArgument(0, new Reference('logger'));
 6   $definition->replaceArgument(1, true);
```

The equivalent in XML would be:

```
 1   <service id="..." class="...">
 2     <argument type="service" id="logger" />
 3     <argument>true</argument>
 4   </service>
```

Tags

There is another thing you may want to do when working with Definition objects: adding tags to them. A tag consists of the name of the tag and an array of attributes. A definition can have multiple tags with the same tag name:

```
1   $definition->addTag('kernel.event_listener', array(
2       'event' => 'kernel.request'
3   );
4   $definition->addTag('kernel.event_listener', array(
5       'event' => 'kernel.response'
6   );
```

In XML you would write this like:

```
1   <service id="..." class="...">
2     <tag name="kernel.event_listener" event="kernel.request">
3     <tag name="kernel.event_listener" event="kernel.response">
4   </service>
```

Aliases

Before talking about what you can do with all this knowledge, there is one last thing you'll need: creating aliases for services:

```
1   $container->setAlias('some_alias', 'some_service_id');
```

Now whenever you request the service some_alias, you will in fact get the service some_-service_id.

6.6 The `Configuration` class

Before we continue, I need to explain a few things about the Configuration class. You may have noticed it earlier, and maybe you have even created one yourself.

Most of the times you will use a Configuration class to define all the possible configuration options for your bundle (though the Config Component is highly decoupled so you can also use anything described below in an entirely different context). The name of the class or its namespace is actually irrelevant, as long as it implements ConfigurationInterface:

```
1   use Symfony\Component\Config\Definition\ConfigurationInterface;
2   use Symfony\Component\Config\Definition\Builder\TreeBuilder;
3
4   class Configuration implements ConfigurationInterface
5   {
6       public function getConfigTreeBuilder()
7       {
8           $treeBuilder = new TreeBuilder();
9           $rootNode = $treeBuilder->root('name_of_bundle');
10
```

```
11        $rootNode
12            ->children()
13                // define configuration nodes
14                ...
15            ->end()
16        ;
17
18        return $treeBuilder;
19    }
20 }
```

There is one public method: `getConfigTreeBuilder()`. This method should return a `TreeBuilder` instance which is a builder you use to describe all configuration options, including their validation rules. Creating a config tree starts with defining a root node:

```
1 $rootNode = $treeBuilder->root('name_of_bundle');
```

The name of the root node should be the name of the bundle, without "bundle", but lower-cased and with underscores. So the node name for `MatthiasAccountBundle` will be `matthias_account`.

The root node is an array node. It can have any child node you like:

```
1 $rootNode
2    ->children()
3        ->booleanNode('auto_connect')
4            ->defaultTrue()
5        ->end()
6        ->scalarNode('default_connection')
7            ->defaultValue('default')
8        ->end()
9    ->end()
10 ;
```

 Learn to write great config trees

When you want to become a proficient bundle creator, practice a lot with defining these config nodes. Your bundle configurations will be much better and very flexible. Read more about the configuration nodes in the documentation of the Config Component[2]. Also take a look at `Configuration` class from existing bundles and try to follow their example.

Usually, you will use an instance of the `Configuration` class inside a bundle's extension class, to process a given set of configuration arrays. These configuration arrays have been collected by the kernel, by loading all the relevant configuration files (like `config_dev.yml`, `config.yml`, `parameters.yml`, etc.).

---

[2]http://symfony.com/doc/current/components/config/definition.html

```
1   class MatthiasAccountExtension extends Extension
2   {
3       public function load(array $configs, ContainerBuilder $container)
4       {
5           $processedConfig = $this->processConfiguration(
6               new Configuration(),
7               $configs
8           );
9       }
10  }
```

The processConfiguration() method of the Extension class instantiates a Processor and finalizes the config tree retrieved from the Configuration object. It then asks the processor to process (validate and merge) the raw configuration arrays:

```
1   final protected function processConfiguration(
2       ConfigurationInterface $configuration,
3       array $configs
4   ) {
5       $processor = new Processor();
6
7       return $processor->processConfiguration($configuration, $configs);
8   }
```

When there were no validation errors, you can then use the configuration values in any way you like. You can define or modify container parameters or service definitions based on the configuration values. In the following chapters we will discuss many different ways to do this.

6.7 Dynamically add tags

Say you want to create a generic event listener, which listens to a configurable list of events, like kernel.request, kernel.response, etc. This is what your Configuration class might look like:

```
1   use Symfony\Component\Config\Definition\ConfigurationInterface;
2
3   class Configuration implements ConfigurationInterface
4   {
5       public function getConfigTreeBuilder()
6       {
7           $treeBuilder = new TreeBuilder();
8           $rootNode = $treeBuilder->root('generic_listener');
9
10          $rootNode
```

```
11              ->children()
12                  ->arrayNode('events')
13                      ->prototype('scalar')
14                      ->end()
15                  ->end()
16              ->end()
17          ;
18
19          return $treeBuilder;
20      }
21  }
```

It allows a list of event names to be configured like this:

```
1  generic_listener:
2      events: [kernel.request, kernel.response, ...]
```

The standard way to register an event listener would be to add tags to the event listener's service definition in services.xml:

```
1  <service id="generic_event_listener" class="...">
2    <tag name="kernel.event_listener" event="..." method="onEvent" />
3    <tag name="kernel.event_listener" event="..." method="onEvent" />
4  </service>
```

But in this situation, we don't know in advance to which events the listener should listen, so these events can not be defined in a configuration file. Luckily - as we saw earlier - we can add tags to service definitions on the fly. This can be done inside the container extension:

```
1  class GenericListenerExtension extends Extension
2  {
3      public function load(array $configs, ContainerBuilder $container)
4      {
5          $processedConfig = $this->processConfiguration(
6              new Configuration(),
7              $configs
8          );
9
10         // load services.xml
11         $loader = ...;
12         $loader->load('services.xml');
13
14         $eventListener = $container
15             ->getDefinition('generic_event_listener');
```

```
16
17          foreach ($processedConfig['events'] as $eventName) {
18              // add a kernel.event_listener tag for each event
19              $eventListener
20                  ->addTag('kernel.event_listener', array(
21                      'event' => $eventName,
22                      'method' => 'onEvent'
23                  ));
24          }
25      }
26  }
```

There is one extra step you might take to prevent a dangling listener service when there are no events to which it should listen:

```
1   if (empty($processedConfig['events'])) {
2       $container->removeDefinition('generic_event_listener');
3   }
```

6.8 Strategy pattern for loading exclusive services

Often bundles provide multiple ways of doing a single thing. For instance, a bundle that provides some kind of mailbox functionality may have different storage implementations, like one storage manager for Doctrine ORM and one for MongoDB. To make the choice for a specific storage manager configurable, create a Configuration class like this:

```
1   use Symfony\Component\Config\Definition\ConfigurationInterface;
2
3   class Configuration implements ConfigurationInterface
4   {
5       public function getConfigTreeBuilder()
6       {
7           $treeBuilder = new TreeBuilder();
8           $rootNode = $treeBuilder->root('browser');
9
10          $rootNode
11              ->children()
12                  ->scalarNode('storage_manager')
13                      ->validate()
14                          ->ifNotInArray(array('doctrine_orm', 'mongo_db')
15                          ->thenInvalid('Invalid storage manager')
16                      ->end()
17                  ->end()
```

```
18              ->end()
19          ;
20
21          return $treeBuilder;
22      }
23  }
```

Then given there are two service definition files for each of the storage managers, like doctrine_-orm.xml:

```
1  <services>
2      <service id="mailbox.doctrine_orm.storage_manager" class="...">
3      </service>
4  </services>
```

And mongo_db.xml:

```
1  <services>
2      <service id="mailbox.mongo_db.storage_manager" class="...">
3      </service>
4  </services>
```

You could then load either of these files by doing something like this in your container extension:

```
1  class MailboxExtension extends Extension
2  {
3      public function load(array $configs, ContainerBuilder $container)
4      {
5          $processedConfig = $this->processConfiguration(
6              new Configuration(),
7              $configs
8          );
9
10         // create an XmlLoader
11         $loader = ...;
12
13         // load only the services for the given storage manager
14         $storageManager = $processedConfig['storage_manager'];
15         $loader->load($storageManager.'.xml');
16
17         // make the specific storage manager available as the general one
18         $container->setAlias(
19             'mailbox.storage_manager',
20             'mailbox.'.$storageManager.'.storage_manager'
```

```
21              );
22          }
23    }
```

A convenient alias is created in the end to allow other parts of the application to just request the `mailbox.storage_manager` service, instead of worrying about the storage-specific service that should be used. However, the way this is done is too rigid: the id of each specific storage manager service should conform to the pattern `mailbox.{storageManagerName}.storage_manager`. It would be better to define the alias inside the service definition files themselves:

```
1    <services>
2      <service id="mailbox.doctrine_orm.storage_manager" class="...">
3      </service>
4
5      <service id="storage_manager"
6        alias="mailbox.doctrine_orm.storage_manager">
7      </service>
8    </services>
```

Using the strategy pattern for loading service definitions has many advantages:

- Only the services that are useful in the current application will be loaded. When you don't have a MongoDB server up and running, there will be no services that accidentally refer to it.
- The setup is open for extension, since you can add the name of another storage manager to the list in the `Configuration` class and then add a service definition file with the necessary services and an alias.

6.9 Loading and configuring additional services

Say you have a bundle dedicated to input filtering. Probably you offer several different services, like services for filtering form data, and services for filtering data stored using Doctrine ORM. It should be possible to enable or disable any of these services or collections of services at any time because they may not all be applicable to your specific situation. There is a handy shortcut for configuration definitions to accomplish a thing like this:

```
1   class Configuration implements ConfigurationInterface
2   {
3       public function getConfigTreeBuilder()
4       {
5           $treeBuilder = new TreeBuilder();
6           $rootNode = $treeBuilder->root('input_filter');
7
8           $rootNode
9               ->children()
10                  ->arrayNode('form_integration')
11                      // will be enabled by default
12                      ->canBeDisabled()
13                  ->end()
14                  ->arrayNode('doctrine_orm_integration')
15                      // will be disabled by default
16                      ->canBeEnabled()
17                  ->end()
18              ->end()
19          ;
20
21          return $treeBuilder;
22      }
23  }
```

With a configuration tree like this, you can enable or disable specific parts of the bundle in `config.yml`:

```
1   input_filter:
2       form_integration:
3           enabled: false
4       doctrine_orm_integration:
5           enabled: true
```

Inside your container extension you can then load the appropriate services:

```
1    class InputFilterExtension extends Extension
2    {
3        public function load(array $configs, ContainerBuilder $container)
4        {
5            $processedConfig = $this->processConfiguration(
6                new Configuration(),
7                $configs
8            );
9
10           if ($processedConfig['doctrine_orm_integration']['enabled']) {
11               $this->loadDoctrineORMIntegration(
12                   $container,
13                   $processedConfig['doctrine_orm_integration']
14               );
15           }
16
17           if ($processedConfig['form_integration']['enabled']) {
18               $this->loadFormIntegration(
19                   $container,
20                   $processedConfig['form_integration']
21               );
22           }
23
24           ...
25       }
26
27       private function loadDoctrineORMIntegration(
28           ContainerBuilder $container,
29           array $configuration
30       ) {
31           // load services, etc.
32           ...
33       }
34
35       private function loadFormIntegration(
36           ContainerBuilder $container,
37           array $configuration
38       ) {
39           ...
40       }
41   }
```

Each of the stand-alone parts of the bundle can be loaded separately like this.

A cleaner configuration class

One or two of these stand-alone bundle parts can be easily handled, but soon the `Configuration` class will contain many lines of code in just one method. You can clean this up a bit by using the `append()` method in combination with some private methods:

```
class Configuration implements ConfigurationInterface
{
    public function getConfigTreeBuilder()
    {
        $treeBuilder = new TreeBuilder();

        $rootNode = $treeBuilder->root('input_filter');

        $rootNode
            ->append($this->createFormIntegrationNode())
            ->append($this->createDoctrineORMIntegrationNode())
        ;

        return $treeBuilder;
    }

    private function createDoctrineORMIntegrationNode()
    {
        $builder = new TreeBuilder();

        $node = $builder->root('doctrine_orm_integration');

        $node
            ->canBeEnabled()
            ->children()
                // maybe add some more configuration
                ...
            ->end();

        return $node;
    }

    private function createFormIntegrationNode()
    {
        ...
    }
}
```

6.10 Configure which services to use

Instead of using the Strategy pattern for loading services you may also allow developers to manually configure a service they want to use. For example, if your bundle needs some kind of encrypter service and the bundle does not provide one itself, you would want to ask the developer to provide the encrypter by its service id:

```
1   matthias_security:
2       encrypter_service: my_encrypter_service_id
```

Your Configuration class should then look like this:

```
1   class Configuration implements ConfigurationInterface
2   {
3       public function getConfigTreeBuilder()
4       {
5           $treeBuilder = new TreeBuilder();
6           $rootNode = $treeBuilder->root('matthias_security');
7
8           $rootNode
9               ->children()
10                  ->scalarNode('encrypter_service')
11                      ->isRequired()
12                  ->end()
13              ->end()
14          ;
15
16          return $treeBuilder;
17      }
18  }
```

Inside the bundle's extension class, you could then create an alias for the configured service.

```
1   class MatthiasSecurityExtension extends Extension
2   {
3       public function load(array $configs, ContainerBuilder $container)
4       {
5           $processedConfig = $this->processConfiguration(
6               new Configuration(),
7               $configs
8           );
9
10          $container->setAlias(
```

```
11                    'matthias_security.encrypter',
12                    $processedConfig['encrypter_service']
13                );
14        }
15   }
```

So even though the service id of the encrypter may originally be anything, now you have a stable reference to it - an alias - which you can use inside any of your bundle's service definitions:

```
1   <service id="matthias_security.encrypted_data_manager" class="...">
2     <argument type="service" id="matthias_security.encrypter" />
3   </service>
```

Of course the assumption here is that the manually configured encrypter service is a valid encrypter object. You can not be sure at configuration time that this is true, so you will have to verify this at runtime. The usual way to do this would be to add the appropriate type-hint to classes of services that use the encrypter service:

```
1   class EncryptedDataManager
2   {
3       public function __construct(EncrypterInterface $encrypter)
4       {
5           // $encrypter is a valid encrypter
6       }
7   }
```

6.11 Completely dynamic service definitions

There are situations when you know almost nothing about the services you need, until you have processed the configuration. Say you want the users of your bundle to define a set of resources as services. These resources can be of type directory or file. You want to create these services on the fly since they differ per application and you need to collect them using a custom service tag, called resource. Your Configuration class may look like this:

```
1   class Configuration implements ConfigurationInterface
2   {
3       public function getConfigTreeBuilder()
4       {
5           $treeBuilder = new TreeBuilder();
6           $rootNode = $treeBuilder->root('resource_management');
7
8           $rootNode
9               ->children()
10                  ->arrayNode('resources')
11                      ->prototype('array')
12                          ->children()
13                              ->scalarNode('type')
14                                  ->validate()
15                                      ->ifNotInArray(
16                                          array('directory', 'file')
17                                      )
18                                      ->thenInvalid('Invalid type')
19                                  ->end()
20                              ->end()
21                              ->scalarNode('path')
22                              ->end()
23                          ->end()
24                      ->end()
25                  ->end()
26              ->end()
27          ;
28
29          return $treeBuilder;
30      }
31  }
```

An example resource configuration:

```
1  resource_management:
2      resources:
3          global_templates:
4              type: directory
5              path: Resources/views
6          app_kernel:
7              type: file
8              path: AppKernel.php
```

When the resources are defined like this, you can create service definitions for them in the container extension:

```
1  class ResourceManagementExtension extends Extension
2  {
3      public function load(array $configs, ContainerBuilder $container)
4      {
5          $processedConfig = $this->processConfiguration(
6              new Configuration(),
7              $configs
8          );
9
10         $resources = $processedConfig['resources'];
11
12         foreach ($resources as $name => $resource) {
13             $this->addResourceDefinition($container, $name, $resource);
14         }
15     }
16
17     private function addResourceDefinition(
18         ContainerBuilder $container,
19         $name,
20         array $resource
21     ) {
22         // determine the class
23         $class = $this->getResourceClass($resource['type']);
24
25         $definition = new Definition($class);
26
27         // add a specific tag
28         $definition->addTag('resource');
29
30         $serviceId = 'resource.'.$name;
31
```

```
32          $container->setDefinition($serviceId, $definition);
33      }
34
35      private function getResourceClass($type)
36      {
37          if ($type === 'directory') {
38              return 'Resource\Directory';
39          } elseif ($type === 'file') {
40              return 'Resource\File';
41          }
42
43          throw new \InvalidArgumentException('Type not supported');
44      }
45  }
```

When these manually created service definitions need arguments, method calls, etc. use the techniques described above to add these dynamically too.

7 Parameter patterns

The service container has service definitions and parameters. Parameters are simple values that can consist of constant scalar values and arrays, in any combination. So `'matthias'` would be a valid parameter, and so would 23 be. But also `array(23 => 'matthias')`, `array(23 => array('matthias'))`, etc.

You can define parameters using the key of your choice. The naming convention however would be: `name_of_your_bundle_without_bundle.parameter_name`. These parameters can be defined in various places.

7.1 `Parameters.yml`

Some of the more essential parameters of your application (which probably have no default value) can be found in `/app/config/parameters.yml`. Parameters are loaded together with service definitions and configuration values for container extensions. That is why the standard `config.yml` starts with these lines:

```
1  imports:
2      - { resource: parameters.yml }
3      - { resource: security.yml }
4
5  framework:
6      secret:            %secret%
7      ...
```

First `parameters.yml` and `security.yml` will be imported. The file `parameters.yml` starts with:

```
1  parameters:
2      database_driver: pdo_mysql
3      ...
```

And `security.yml` starts with:

```
1  security:
2      encoders:
3          Symfony\Component\Security\Core\User\User: plaintext
4      ...
```

These files will be imported as they are. So `config.yml` could just as well look like:

```
1  parameters:
2      ...
3  security:
4      ...
5  framework:
6      ...
```

Since all configuration arrays will be merged in the end, it is possible in config.yml to override any parameter defined in parameters.yml:

```
1  parameters:
2      ... # loaded from parameters.yml
3      database_driver: pdo_sqlite
```

Even service definitions can be created within config.yml (or any service container configuration file for that matter):

```
1  parameters:
2      ...
3  services:
4      some_service_id:
5          class: SomeClass
```

7.2 Parameter resolving

Values defined in config.yml, or parameters.yml but also in service definitions and definition arguments can contain placeholders for values that should have been defined as parameters. When the service container gets compiled, values containing placeholders will be resolved. For instance in the example above we defined the database_driver parameter in parameters.yml. In config.yml we can refer to this parameter using the %database_driver% placeholder:

```
1  doctrine:
2      dbal:
3          driver: %database_driver%
```

When creating service definitions, the Symfony bundles usually take the same approach when it comes to the class names used:

```
1  <parameters>
2      <parameter key="form.factory.class">
3          Symfony\Component\Form\FormFactory
4      </parameter>
5  </parameters>
6
7  <service id="form.factory" class="%form.factory.class%">
8  </service>
```

Parameters for class names

Using parameters for class names would allow other parts of the application to replace the parameter, instead of directly modifying the service definition. It is not very likely however that this will happen, and when every service definition has its class in a parameter, this parameter also ends up in the final service container, so that even at runtime you could call $container->getParameter('form.factory.class') and retrieve the class name of the form factory. This seems very redundant to me and I would not recommend it when creating your own service definitions.

Whenever you would want to change the class of a definition, you could do this inside a compiler pass:

```php
1  use Symfony\Component\DependencyInjection\ContainerBuilder;
2  use Symfony\Component\DependencyInjection\Compiler\CompilerPassInterface;
3
4  class ReplaceClassCompilerPass implements CompilerPassInterface
5  {
6      public function process(ContainerBuilder $container)
7      {
8          $myCustomFormFactoryClass = ...;
9
10         $container
11             ->getDefinition('form.factory')
12             ->setClass($myCustomFormFactoryClass);
13     }
14 }
```

Manually resolving parameters

When you are using parameters in your bundle extension (or in a compiler pass), the values of these parameters are not fully resolved yet. For example, your bundle may define a parameter my_cache_-dir, referring to the %kernel.cache_dir% which contains the location of the cache directory used by the kernel:

```
1  parameters:
2      my_cache_dir: %kernel.cache_dir%/my_cache
```

In the load() method of your container extension you would like to create this directory if it
does not already exist:

```
1  class MyExtension extends Extension
2  {
3      public function load(array $configs, ContainerBuilder $container)
4      {
5          $myCacheDir = $container->getParameter('my_cache_dir');
6
7          ...
8      }
9  }
```

When the load() method gets called, the my_cache_dir parameter is still literally "%ker-
nel.cache_dir%/my_cache". Luckily you can use the ParameterBag::resolveValue() method to
replace all placeholders with their current values:

```
1  $myCacheDir = $container->getParameter('my_cache_dir');
2
3  $myCacheDir = $container->getParameterBag()->resolveValue($myCacheDir);
4
5  // now you can create the cache directory
6  mkdir($myCacheDir);
```

Kernel parameters

By itself, the kernel adds these parameters to the container, before loading the bundles:

`kernel.root_dir`
The location of the kernel class (e.g. `/app`)

`kernel.environment`
The environment (e.g. `dev`, `prod`, etc.)

`kernel.debug`
Debug mode (`true` or `false`)

`kernel.name`
The name of the directory the kernel is in (e.g. `app`)

`kernel.cache_dir`
The location of the cache directory (e.g. `/app/cache/dev`)

`kernel.logs_dir`
the location of the logs directory (e.g. `/app/logs`)

`kernel.bundles`
a list of enabled bundles (e.g. `array('FrameworkBundle' =>
'Symfony\\Bundle\\FrameworkBundle\\FrameworkBundle', ...)`,

`kernel.charset`
the character set used for responses (e.g. `UTF-8`)

`kernel.container_class`
the name of the service container class (e.g. `appDevDebugProjectContainer`), to be found in `kernel.cache_dir`.

The kernel also adds any environment variable that starts with `SYMFONY__`. Before doing so, it replaces `__` with `.` in the names of these variables, so `SYMFONY__DATABASE__USER` will be available as the `database.user` parameter.

7.3 Define parameters in a container extension

Many times you will find yourself in the following situation:

- You want the developer to provide some value for your bundle's configuration in `config.yml`.
- You then need to use this specific value as an argument for one of the services of your bundle.

Say you have a `BrowserBundle` and you want the developer to provide a `timeout` value for the `browser` service:

```
1  browser:
2      timeout: 30
```

Your bundle's Configuration class should look like:

```
1  class Configuration implements ConfigurationInterface
2  {
3      public function getConfigTreeBuilder()
4      {
5          $treeBuilder = new TreeBuilder();
6          $rootNode = $treeBuilder->root('browser');
7
8          $rootNode
9              ->children()
10                 ->scalarNode('timeout')
11                 ->end()
12             ->end()
13         ;
14
15         return $treeBuilder;
16 }
```

Then inside your container extension you need to process the configuration values from config.yml and the likes:

```
1  class BrowserExtension extends Extension
2  {
3      public function load(array $configs, ContainerBuilder $container)
4      {
5          // load the service definitions
6          $fileLocator = new FileLocator(__DIR__.'/../Resources/config');
7          $loader = new XmlFileLoader($container, $fileLocator);
8          $loader->load('services.xml');
9
10         // process the configuration
11         $processedConfig = $this->processConfiguration(
12             new Configuration(),
13             $configs
14         );
15     }
16 }
```

Your browser service is defined in services.xml:

```
1  <service id="browser" class="...">
2    <argument>%browser.timeout%</argument>
3  </service>
```

The value for timeout that the user has provided in `config.yml` ("30") will be available in the container extension's `load()` method as `$processedConfig['timeout']` so the only thing you need to do in that method is copy this value as a parameter to the service container:

```
1  $container->setParameter('browser.timeout', $processedConfig['timeout']);
```

7.4 Override parameters with a compiler pass

Sometimes you want to analyze and override a parameter defined in another bundle, after this bundle has had the chance to define it. For example you may want to modify the hierarchy of user roles defined in `security.yml`, which will be available as the container parameter `security.role_-hierarchy.roles`. This is the standard hierarchy:

```
1  array (
2    'ROLE_ADMIN' =>
3      array (
4        0 => 'ROLE_USER',
5      ),
6    'ROLE_SUPER_ADMIN' =>
7      array (
8        0 => 'ROLE_USER',
9        1 => 'ROLE_ADMIN',
10       2 => 'ROLE_ALLOWED_TO_SWITCH',
11     ),
12 )
```

Say you have another mechanism for determining a role hierarchy (maybe you retrieve them from some other configuration file), you can then modify or replace the role hierarchy entirely by creating a dedicated compiler pass:

```
 1  class EnhanceRoleHierarchyPass implements CompilerPassInterface
 2  {
 3      public function process(ContainerBuilder $container)
 4      {
 5          $parameterName = 'security.role_hierarchy.roles';
 6
 7          $roleHierarchy = $container->getParameter($parameterName);
 8
 9          // modify the role hierarchy
10          ...
11
12          $container->setParameter($parameterName, $roleHierarchy);
13      }
14  }
```

Don't forget to register this compiler pass in your bundle class:

```
 1  class YourBundle extends Bundle
 2  {
 3      public function build(ContainerBuilder $container)
 4      {
 5          $container->addCompilerPass(new EnhanceRoleHierarchyPass());
 6      }
 7  }
```

 Service definition validation

When something is wrong with a service definition, in many cases you will only notice it when you actually run the application.

To receive warnings about invalid service definitions early on, install the SymfonyServiceDefinitionValidator[1] and enable its compiler pass. From then on, when the service container is being compiled, you automatically get error messages for any problem that can be spotted at compile time, like service definitions with non-existing classes or calls to methods that don't exist. The validator even recognizes bad constructor arguments.

---

[1]https://github.com/matthiasnoback/symfony-service-definition-validator

III Project structure

In the previous parts we looked at the inner workings of the kernel which creates a response for each request. We also discussed at great length any way in which you can write highly configurable bundles. With that knowledge, you can make your code available as services for other parts of the application. When it comes to structuring entire applications, there are still some questions remaining. How can you prevent all the code from ending up in controller classes? How can you write code that enables reusability *within* your project? And how can you write code that can be called from the web and from the command line?

8 Organizing application layers

8.1 Slim controllers

In many Symfony applications, controller code ends up looking like this:

```php
namespace Matthias\AccountBundle\Controller;

use Symfony\Bundle\FrameworkBundle\Controller;
use Symfony\Component\HttpFoundation\Request;
use Matthias\AccountBundle\Entity\Account;

class AccountController extends Controller
{
    public function newAction(Request $request)
    {
        $account = new Account();

        $form = $this->createForm(new AccountType(), $account);

        if ($request->isMethod('POST')) {
            $form->bind($request);

            if ($form->isValid()) {
                $confirmationCode = $this
                    ->get('security.secure_random')
                    ->nextBytes(4);
                $account
                    ->setConfirmationCode(md5($confirmationCode));

                $entityManager = $this->getDoctrine()->getManager();
                $entityManager->persist($account);
                $entityManager->flush();

                $this->sendAccountConfirmationMessage($account);

                return $this->redirect($this->generateUrl('mailbox_index'));
            }
        }
```

```
35        return array(
36            'form' => $form->createView(),
37        );
38    }
39
40    private function sendAccountConfirmationMessage(Account $account)
41    {
42        $message = \Swift_Message::newInstance()
43            ->setSubject('Confirm account')
44            ->setFrom('noreply@matthias.com')
45            ->setTo($account->getEmailAddress())
46            ->setBody('Welcome! ...');
47
48        $this->get('mailer')->send($message);
49    }
50 }
```

When you look at the newAction controller you can see that there is a form type AccountType, the data class of which is Matthias\AccountBundle\Entity\Account. After binding and validating the form, a confirmation code will be generated, and the account object will be persisted. Then a confirmation mail is being created and sent.

There is *too much* going on here, the result of which is that:

1. It is impossible to separate reusable code from project-specific code here. Suppose you want to reuse part of the account creation logic in a future project. This is only be possible by copy-pasting the code from this controller into your new project. This is called **immobility**: code can not be easily transferred to another application.

2. It is also impossible to reuse account creation logic in some other part of this application, since everything is written inline, inside the controller. Let's say you have to create a console command for importing a CSV file containing account data of users of an older version of the application. You have no way to build such a thing without (again) copy-pasting part of the code to another class. I call this **controller-centrism** - code is too much formed around a controller.

3. The code is tightly coupled to two other libraries: SwiftMailer and Doctrine ORM. It is impossible to run this code without either of them, even though there are many alternatives for both. This is called **tight coupling** and is generally not a good thing.

In order to be able to reuse code in another application, or to reuse code in another *part* of the same application, or to switch from mailer or storage manager implementation, you need to split the code into multiple classes with single responsibilities.

8.2 Form handlers

The first step is: delegating the form handling to a specialized form handler. This form handler is a very simple class, which processes the form and does whatever is expected. The result of the first refactoring is the CreateAccountFormHandler:

```php
namespace Matthias\AccountBundle\Form\Handler;

use Symfony\Component\HttpFoundation\Request;
use Symfony\Component\Form\FormInterface;
use Doctrine\ORM\EntityManager;
use Matthias\AccountBundle\Entity\Account;
use Symfony\Component\Security\Core\Util\SecureRandomInterface;

class CreateAccountFormHandler
{
    private $entityManager;
    private $secureRandom;

    public function __construct(
        EntityManager $entityManager,
        SecureRandomInterface $secureRandom
    ) {
        $this->entityManager = $entityManager;
        $this->secureRandom = $secureRandom;
    }

    public function handle(FormInterface $form, Request $request)
    {
        if (!$request->isMethod('POST')) {
            return false;
        }

        $form->bind($request);

        if (!$form->isValid()) {
            return false;
        }

        $validAccount = $form->getData();

        $this->createAccount($validAccount);
```

```
38          return true;
39      }
40
41      private function createAccount(Account $account)
42      {
43          $confirmationCode = $this
44              ->secureRandom
45              ->nextBytes(4);
46
47          $account
48              ->setConfirmationCode(md5($confirmationCode));
49
50          $this->entityManager->persist($account);
51          $this->entityManager->flush();
52      }
53 }
```

The service definition for this form handler would look like:

```
1 <service id="matthias_account.create_account_form_handler"
2   class="Matthias\AccountBundle\Form\Handler\CreateAccountFormHandler">
3   <argument type="service" id="entity_manager" />
4   <argument type="service" id="security.secure_random" />
5 </service>
```

As you can see, the handle() method returns true if it was able to do everything it intended to do, and false if anything went wrong in the process and the form should be rendered again. Using this simple mechanism, the controller can be slimmed down a lot:

```
1 class AccountController extends Controller
2 {
3      public function newAction(Request $request)
4      {
5          $account = new Account();
6
7          $form = $this->createForm(new AccountType(), $account);
8
9          $formHandler = $this
10              ->get('matthias_account.create_account_form_handler');
11
12          if ($formHandler->handle($form, $request)) {
13              $this->sendAccountConfirmationMessage($account);
14
```

```
15          return $this->redirect($this->generateUrl('mailbox_index'));
16      }
17
18      return array(
19          'form' => $form->createView(),
20      );
21  }
22 }
```

Form handlers should be very simple and should throw no exceptions that are intended as feedback to the user. Any feedback you would want to provide from within the form handler should be created by adding extra form errors to the form and returning `false` to indicate that there was a problem:

```
1  use Symfony\Component\Form\FormError;
2
3  public function handle(FormInterface $form, Request $request)
4  {
5      if (...) {
6          $form->addError(new FormError('There was a problem'));
7
8          return false;
9      }
10 }
```

However, keep in mind that ideally any error related to a form is a validation error. This means that the form handler should not have to do any validation other than calling `isValid()`. Just create any kind of validation constraint[1] and a corresponding validator to ensure that all checks for validity are centrally available and therefore reusable.

8.3 Domain managers

The form handler (and maybe the form type), would be a great candidate for reuse. However, there is still too much happening in the form handler. Considering that the responsibility of a form handler is "to handle a form", it is likely that creating a confirmation code is too much. Also, talking directly to the persistence layer (in this case Doctrine ORM) is too much to ask of a simple form handler.

The solution for this problem is to delegate domain-related tasks to domain managers. These managers may talk directly to the persistence layer. Let's call the domain manager for `Account`-related tasks the `AccountManager`. It would look something like this:

---

[1]http://symfony.com/doc/master/cookbook/validation/custom_constraint.html

```
 1  namespace Matthias\AccountBundle\DomainManager;
 2
 3  use Symfony\Component\HttpFoundation\Request;
 4  use Symfony\Component\Form\FormInterface;
 5  use Doctrine\ORM\EntityManager;
 6  use Matthias\AccountBundle\Entity\Account;
 7  use Symfony\Component\Security\Core\Util\SecureRandomInterface;
 8
 9  class AccountManager
10  {
11      private $entityManager;
12      private $secureRandom;
13
14      public function __construct(
15          EntityManger $entityManager,
16          SecureRandomInterface $secureRandom
17      ) {
18          $this->entityManager = $entityManager;
19          $this->secureRandom = $secureRandom;
20      }
21
22      public function createAccount(Account $account)
23      {
24          $confirmationCode = $this
25              ->secureRandom
26              ->nextBytes(4);
27
28          $account
29              ->setConfirmationCode(md5($confirmationCode));
30
31          $this->entityManager->persist($account);
32          $this->entityManager->flush();
33      }
34  }
```

Now the form handler just uses the AccountManager to really create the account:

```
1  class CreateAccountFormHandler
2  {
3      private $accountManager;
4
5      public function __construct(AccountManager $accountManager)
6      {
7          $this->accountManager = $accountManager;
8      }
9
10     public function handle(FormInterface $form, Request $request)
11     {
12         ...
13
14         $validAccount = $form->getData();
15
16         $this->accountManager->createAccount($validAccount);
17     }
18 }
```

These are the corresponding service definitions for the form handler and domain manager classes:

```
1  <service id="matthias_account.create_account_form_handler"
2    class="Matthias\AccountBundle\Form\Handler\CreateAccountFormHandler">
3    <argument type="service" id="matthias_account.account_manager" />
4  </service>
5
6  <service id="matthias_account.account_manager"
7    class="Matthias\AccountBundle\DomainManager\AccountManager">
8    <argument type="service" id="entity_manager" />
9    <argument type="service" id="security.secure_random" />
10 </service>
```

Domain managers can do anything a domain object itself could not accomplish. You can use it to encapsulate logic about:

- Creating objects and persisting them
- Creating relations between objects (like connecting two users)
- Duplicating objects
- Removing objects
- ...

8.4 Events

As you may have noticed, inside the controller a confirmation mail was sent after creating the new account. Things like this are better off with some delegation. Sending a mail is probably not the only thing that should be done when there is a new account. Maybe some settings object has to be pre-populated with default settings for the new user, or maybe a notification should be sent to the owner of the site that there is a new user of his product.

This is a perfect use-case for an event-driven approach: it seems that inside the `AccountManager` a generic event takes place, (namely, "a new account has been created"). Other parts of the application should be allowed to respond to this fact. In this case there should be at least an event listener that sends the confirmation mail to the new user.

To be able to dispatch a custom event with some specific data you need to create your own event class, which extends from the generic `Event` class:

```php
namespace Matthias\AccountBundle\Event;

use Symfony\Component\EventDispatcher\Event;

class AccountEvent extends Event
{
    private $account;

    public function __construct(Account $account)
    {
        $this->account = $account;
    }

    public function getAccount()
    {
        return $this->account;
    }
}
```

Then we need to think of a name for the event - let's call it `matthias_account.new_account_-created`. It's generally best practice to store this name as a constant of a dedicated class in your bundle:

```
1   namespace Matthias\AccountBundle\Event;
2
3   class AccountEvents
4   {
5       const NEW_ACCOUNT_CREATED = 'matthias_account.new_account_created';
6   }
```

Now we need to modify the AccountManager to actually dispatch this matthias_account.new_-account_created event:

```
1   namespace Matthias\AccountBundle\DomainManager;
2
3   use Symfony\Component\EventDispatcher\EventDispatcherInterface;
4   use Matthias\AccountBundle\Event\AccountEvents;
5   use Matthias\AccountBundle\Event\AccountEvent;
6
7   class AccountManager
8   {
9       ...
10
11      private $eventDispatcher;
12
13      public function __construct(
14          ...
15          EventDispatcherInterface $eventDispatcher
16      ) {
17          ...
18
19          $this->eventDispatcher = $eventDispatcher;
20      }
21
22      public function createAccount(Account $account)
23      {
24          ...
25
26          $this->eventDispatcher->dispatch(
27              AccountEvents::NEW_ACCOUNT_CREATED,
28              new AccountEvent($account)
29          );
30      }
31  }
```

Don't forget to add the event_dispatcher service as an argument to the service definition of the AccountManager:

```
1  <service id="matthias_account.account_manager"
2    class="Matthias\AccountBundle\DomainManager\AccountManager">
3    <argument type="service" id="entity_manager" />
4    <argument type="service" id="security.secure_random" />
5    <argument type="service" id="event_dispatcher" />
6  </service>
```

The event listener for the `matthias_account.new_account_created` event will look like this:

```
1  namespace Matthias\AccountBundle\EventListener;
2
3  use Symfony\Component\EventDispatcher\EventSubscriberInterface;
4  use Matthias\AccountBundle\Event\AccountEvents;
5  use Matthias\AccountBundle\Event\AccountEvent;
6
7  class SendConfirmationMailListener implements EventSubscriberInterface
8  {
9      private $mailer;
10
11     public static function getSubscribedEvents()
12     {
13         return array(
14             AccountEvents::NEW_ACCOUNT_CREATED => 'onNewAccount'
15         );
16     }
17
18     public function __construct(\SwiftMailer $mailer)
19     {
20         $this->mailer = $mailer;
21     }
22
23     public function onNewAccount(AccountEvent $event)
24     {
25         $this->sendConfirmationMessage($event->getAccount());
26     }
27
28     private function sendConfirmationMessage(Account $account)
29     {
30         $message = \Swift_Message::newInstance();
31
32         ...
33
34         $this->mailer->send($message);
```

```
35        }
36   }
```

Since this event listener needs the mailer to do its work, we need to inject it by adding an argument to its service definition. In fact, we also have to add a tag `kernel.event_subscriber` which registers the `SendConfirmationMailListener` as an event subscriber:

```
1   <service id="life_online_account.send_confirmation_mail_listener"
2     class="Matthias\AccountBundle\EventListener\SendConfirmationMailListener">
3     <argument type="service" id="mailer" />
4     <tag name="kernel.event_subscriber" />
5   </service>
```

Event listener best practices

An event listener should be named after the thing it does, not after the event it listens to. So instead of naming an event listener `NewAccountEventListener`, you should name it `SendConfirmationMailListener`. This also helps other developers when they are trying to find the place where a confirmation mail is being sent.

Also, when something else should happen when an event occurs, like sending a mail to the owner of the site, you should create another listener service for it, instead of adding more code to the existing listener. Enabling or disabling specific listeners will be much easier, and maintainability increases, because you won't accidentally change existing behavior.

Persistence events

You may recall that the `AccountManager` (a domain manager) generated a confirmation code for the account, right before persisting it:

```
1   class AccountManager
2   {
3       private $entityManager;
4       private $secureRandom;
5
6       public function __construct(
7           EntityManger $entityManager,
8           SecureRandomInterface $secureRandom
9       ) {
10          $this->entityManager = $entityManager;
11          $this->secureRandom = $secureRandom;
12      }
13
```

```
14      public function createAccount(Account $account)
15      {
16          $confirmationCode = $this
17              ->secureRandom
18              ->nextBytes(4);
19
20          $account
21              ->setConfirmationCode(md5($confirmationCode));
22
23          $this->entityManager->persist($account);
24          $this->entityManager->flush();
25      }
26  }
```

This is not such a good idea. Again: an account may be created in another place and then it will not have a confirmation code at all. From a "responsibility" point of view, looking at the dependencies of the AccountManager, it is quite strange that it should have a SecureRandomInterface object as a dependency: why would it need that, when it just knows how to create an account?

This logic should be moved to some other place, closer to the real event of persisting a new account. Most persistence layers support something like events or behaviors by which you can hook into the process of storing new objects, updating or removing existing objects.

For Doctrine ORM it starts with an event subscriber:

```
1   use Doctrine\Common\EventSubscriber;
2   use Doctrine\ORM\Event\LifecycleEventArgs;
3
4   class CreateConfirmationCodeEventSubscriber implements EventSubscriber
5   {
6       private $secureRandom;
7
8       public function __construct(SecureRandomInterface $secureRandom)
9       {
10          $this->secureRandom = $secureRandom;
11      }
12
13      public function getSubscribedEvents()
14      {
15          return array(
16              'prePersist'
17          );
18      }
19
20      public function prePersist(LifecycleEventArgs $event)
```

```
21      {
22          // this will be called for *each* new entity
23
24          $entity = $event->getEntity();
25          if (!($entity instanceof Account)) {
26              return;
27          }
28
29          $this->createConfirmationCodeFor($entity);
30      }
31
32      private function createConfirmationCodeFor(Account $account)
33      {
34          $confirmationCode = $this
35              ->secureRandom
36              ->nextBytes(4);
37
38          $account
39              ->setConfirmationCode(md5($confirmationCode));
40      }
41  }
```

You can register this event subscriber using the tag doctrine.event_subscriber:

```
1  <service id="create_confirmation_code_listener" class="...">
2    <tag name="doctrine.event_subscriber" />
3  </service>
```

There are more events[2], like postPersist, preUpdate, preFlush, etc. which allow you to respond to many of the important events in the lifecycle of entities. Specifically preUpdate can be very handy, to determine if someone has changed the value of a specific field:

```
1  use Doctrine\ORM\Event\PreUpdateEventArgs;
2
3  class CreateConfirmationCodeEventSubscriber implements EventSubscriber
4  {
5      public function getSubscribedEvents()
6      {
7          return array(
8              'preUpdate'
9          );
10      }
```

---

[2]http://docs.doctrine-project.org/projects/doctrine-orm/en/latest/reference/events.html#listening-and-subscribing-to-lifecycle-events

```
11
12    public function preUpdate(PreUpdateEventArgs $event)
13    {
14        $entity = $event->getEntity();
15        if (!($entity instanceof Account)) {
16            return;
17        }
18
19        if ($event->hasChangedField('emailAddress')) {
20            // create a new confirmation code
21            $confirmationCode = ...;
22            $event->setNewValue('confirmationCode', $confirmationCode);
23        }
24    }
```

As you can see, listeners to the preUpdate event receive a special event object. You can use it to examine which fields have changed and to add some more changes.

 Doctrine event gotchas

Some things that are not immediately clear when it comes to Doctrine events:

- The preUpdate event is *only* dispatched when the value of some field was changed, not necessarily any time you call flush() on the entity manager.
- The prePersist event is *only* dispatched when an entity was not persisted before.
- In certain situations you are too late to make any changes to an object, so when you do, you need to make the UnitOfWork recompute the changes manually:

```
1    $entity = $event->getEntity();
2    $className = get_class($entity);
3    $entityManager = $event->getEntityManager();
4    $classMetadata = $entityManager->getClassMetadata($className);
5    $unitOfWork = $entityManager->getUnitOfWork();
6    $unitOfWork->recomputeSingleEntityChangeSet($classMetadata, $entity);
```

9 State and context

Services can be divided in two groups:

1. Static services
2. Dynamic services

The majority of the services defined in your service container are in the first category. A static service does the same thing over and over again. Maybe the first time a bit more inefficient. But given the same input, it does the same thing and the result will be the same too. Think about sending a mail using the mailer service, or storing an object using an entity manager.

The second category contains services that have some volatility: when you use a dynamic service, you don't know in advance if it works as expected, since it may depend on the current request, or in the case of a Symfony application: on the fact that the kernel is currently handling a request.

9.1 The security context

One obvious example of a dynamic service is the security context. Whether or not it will give you a user object when you call ->getToken()->getUser() on it, depends on many things, especially on the request and if the firewall can derive if there is a user currently logged in. However, many services I've seen, have a dependency on the security context, like this one:

```
1   use Symfony\Component\Security\Core\SecurityContextInterface;
2
3   class UserMailer
4   {
5       private $securityContext;
6       private $mailer;
7
8       public function __construct(
9           SecurityContextInterface $securityContext,
10          \SwiftMailer $mailer
11      ) {
12          $this->securityContext = $securityContext;
13          $this->mailer = $mailer;
14      }
15
16      public function sendMailToCurrentUser($subject, $body)
17      {
18          $token = $this->securityContext->getToken();
```

```
19        if (!($token instanceof TokenInterface)) {
20            // we are not behind a firewall
21            return;
22        }
23
24        $user = $token->getUser();
25        if (!($user instanceof User)) {
26            // no logged in user
27            return;
28        }
29
30        $message = \Swift_Message::newInstance()
31            ->setTo($user->getEmailAddress())
32            ->setSubject($subject)
33            ->setBody($messageBody);
34
35        $this->get('mailer')->send($message);
36    }
37 }
```

The service definition for this class looks like:

```
1 <service id="user_mailer" class="UserMailer">
2   <argument type="service" id="security.context" />
3   <argument type="service" id="mailer" />
4 </service>
```

Inside a controller you can do this to send a message to the current user (the @Secure annotation will make sure there is an authenticated user and he has the role ROLE_USER):

```
1 use Symfony\Bundle\FrameworkBundle\Controller\Controller;
2 use JMS\SecurityExtraBundle\Annotation\Secure;
3
4 class SomeController extends Controller
5 {
6     /**
7      * @Secure("ROLE_USER")
8      */
9     public function sendMailAction()
10    {
11        $this->get('user_mailer')->sendMailToCurrentUser('Hi', 'there!');
12    }
13 }
```

Why is this bad? Well, there we go:

1. The user_mailer service can only be used for sending mails to the current user.

   There is however nothing specific about the current user in comparison with other users. The sendMailToCurrentUser($subject, $body) method could easily be changed to sendMailTo(User $user, $subject, $body). This makes your class much more generic and reusable.

2. The user_mailer service can only be used during the lifetime of a request which is secured by a firewall.

   When requesting the user_mailer from within a console command, the service would therefore be totally useless, even though you may still want to send a message to a user. The solution to the first problem solves this problem without any extra effort.

So let's change the UserMailer class to this:

```
class UserMailer
{
    private $mailer;

    public function __construct(\SwiftMailer $mailer)
    {
        $this->mailer = $mailer;
    }

    public function sendMailToUser(User $user, $subject, $body)
    {
        $message = \Swift_Message::newInstance()
            ->setTo($user->getEmailAddress())
            ->setSubject($subject)
            ->setBody($body);

        $this->mailer->send($message);
    }
}
```

The result is a smaller class and much cleaner code. From now on the user_mailer service has no idea to which user it should send a mail (which is good): you always need to provide a User object, which may or may not be the current user.

The controller is an excellent place to determine the current user, since we know that a controller is only executed during the handling of a request, and we know that it is behind a firewall, when we have explicitly configured it to be. So there should be a "current user" (provided that our firewall configuration is correct) and now we can do this:

```
1   class SomeController extends Controller
2   {
3       /**
4        * @Secure("ROLE_USER")
5        */
6       public function sendMailAction()
7       {
8           $user = $this->getUser();
9
10          $this->get('user_mailer')->sendMailTo($user, 'Hi', 'there!');
11      }
12  }
```

 The current user

Whenever you want to do something in a service *only* for the current user, it's better to provide the user from the outside, as an argument or maybe even using a setter method, then to fetch the user using the SecurityContext inside the service.

9.2 The request

The security context is populated with the user token once per request, but only for the master request. But other services you create may depend on the current Request object, which is different for master and sub-requests. This Request object is available as the request service, which is a dynamic service. There is a time (in fact: before the kernel is asked to handle the request) when this request service is even unavailable and can not be used by any other object as a dependency. In fact, there is also a time when there is more than one request service, namely when the kernel handles a sub-request.

Inside the service container this problem is solved using the notion of *scope*. The container can enter and leave scopes and at the moment of the transition between scopes, the previous service will be recovered, or a new service should be provided for the new scope. In the case of the request service, these are the executive states the container will be in:

1. The container is in container scope, the request service is undefined.
2. The kernel handles the main request, it instructs the container to enter the request scope and sets the request service.
3. The kernel handles a sub-request, it instructs the container to enter a new request scope and sets the sub-request as the request service.
4. The kernel finishes the sub-request, it instructs the container to leave the request scope. The previous request service will be restored.

5. The kernel finishes the main request and instructs the container to leave the request scope. The request service will be undefined again.

This way, whenever you call $container->get('request') you "always" retrieve the current Request object. When you need to have the request service available in one of your own objects, there are multiple ways[1] to do this which I all **strongly discourage**.

It is not evil per se to need the request to be able to perform a certain action. But you should not depend on the request *as a service*. Say you want to do something like logging access to pages:

```
use Symfony\Component\HttpFoundation\Request;

class PageCounter
{
    private $counter;

    public function __construct(Request $request)
    {
        $this->request = $request;
    }

    public function incrementPageCounter()
    {
        $uri = $this->request->getPathInfo();

        // somehow increment the page counter for this URI
        ...
    }
}
```

With the corresponding service definition:

```
<service id="page_counter" class="PageCounter" scope="request">
  <argument type="service" id="request" />
</service>
```

Since you depend on the request service, your entire service itself should also have the scope request.

Inside a controller you would now call:

---

[1]http://symfony.com/doc/current/cookbook/service_container/scopes.html

```
1   class InterestingController extends Controller
2   {
3       public function indexAction()
4       {
5           $this->get('page_counter')->incrementPageCounter();
6       }
7   }
```

Of course the page_counter service is able to find out the URI of the current page since it has the entire Request object. But now:

1. Statistics can only be gathered *during* the current request.

   When the kernel is done with handling the request, the request service itself will be set to null and the page counter becomes useless.

2. The PageCounter class is now tightly coupled to the Request class.

   The counter only needs to have some URI. This URI does not necessarily have to come from a Request object. It would be better to pass it as an argument to the incrementPageCounter() method:

```
1   public function incrementPageCounter($uri)
2   {
3       ...
4   }
```

These two problems can seem far-fetched. But it is very probable that one day you need to import old page count data collected in some other way, and then you need to manually call the incrementPageCounter(). It will then help you very much that it is not so tightly coupled to the Request class.

Avoiding a dependency on the current request

There are two major strategies for avoiding your services to be somehow dependent on the current request:

Use an event listener

As you may remember from the first chapter: the kernel always dispatches a kernel.request event for each request it handles. At that moment, you can use an event listener to do something that you want to do for every request, like increment a page counter, or maybe prevent further execution by throwing an exception[2].

---

[2]http://php-and-symfony.matthiasnoback.nl/2012/12/prevent-controller-execution-with-annotations-and-return-a-custom-response/

```
1   class PageCounterListener
2   {
3       private $counter;
4
5       public function __construct(PageCounter $counter)
6       {
7           $this->counter = $counter;
8       }
9
10      public function onKernelRequest(GetResponseEvent $event)
11      {
12          $request = $event->getRequest();
13
14          $this->counter->incrementPageCounter($request->getPathInfo());
15      }
16  }
```

Providing the request object at runtime

When you do need the entire Request object it is always better to start from a place where you *know* this object exists (and you can retrieve it reliably) and from that moment on pass it around to other services:

```
1   class SomeController extends Controller
2   {
3       public function indexAction(Request $request)
4       {
5           $this->get('page_counter')->handle($request);
6       }
7   }
```

Request matchers

In many situations in which you need the `Request` object inside your service, you might use it to perform some kind of matching on it. You could then abstract the matching logic using a request matcher:

```
1   use Symfony\Component\HttpFoundation\RequestMatcherInterface;
2   use Symfony\Component\HttpFoundation\Request;
3
4   class MyRequestMatcher implements RequestMatcherInterface
5   {
6       public function matches(Request $request)
7       {
8           return $request->getClientIp() === '127.0.0.1';
9       }
10  }
```

Or use the standard `RequestMatcher`:

```
1   use Symfony\Component\HttpFoundation\RequestMatcher;
2
3   $matcher = new RequestMatcher();
4   $matcher->matchIp('127.0.0.1');
5   // $matcher->matchPath('^/secure');
6   ...
7
8   if ($matcher->matches($request)) {
9       ...
10  }
```

Using specific values only

Before passing through an entire `Request` object, always ask yourself: do I really need all this information? Or do I need only one particular bit? If so, decouple your class from the `Request` class and adapt the arguments:

Change this:

```
 1  class AccessLogger
 2  {
 3      public function logAccess(Request $request)
 4      {
 5          $ipAddress = $request->getClientIp();
 6
 7          // log the IP address
 8          ...
 9      }
10  }
```

Into:

```
1  class AccessLogger
2  {
3      public function logAccess($ipAddress)
4      {
5          ...
6      }
7  }
```

This makes your code reusable in other projects that don't use the Symfony HttpFoundation Component. See also Reduce coupling to the framework.

IV Configuration conventions

10 Application configuration setup

The Symfony Standard Edition recommends the use of a parameters.yml file to contain configuration values that are specific for an instance of the project, be it on a production server or on the developer's computer. The configuration values defined in config.yml contain placeholders, pointing to parameters in parameters.yml, which are loaded in the imports section:

```
1  imports:
2      - { resource: parameters.yml }
3
4  doctrine:
5      dbal:
6          user:     %database_user%
7          password: %database_password%
```

In parameters.yml you should then define:

```
1  parameters:
2      database_user:     matthias
3      database_password: cookies
```

Or you will get a nasty exception when you run the application:

```
1  You have requested a non-existent parameter "database_user".
```

This set-up soon gets impractical. The more dependencies you have in your project, the more configuration values will differ between you and your colleagues (let alone between your machine and the production server). So the list in parameters.yml gets longer and longer and every time a team member adds another parameter to the list, you will get another ParameterNotFoundException after pulling the changes from the repository.

This method is also very inflexible when you want to change the behavior of some bundles without making these changes permanent. Chances are you will accidentally commit things like:

```
1  # in config.yml
2  swiftmailer:
3      # deliver all emails sent by the application to this address:
4      delivery_address: matthiasnoback@gmail.com
```

Of course you can define another parameter for it:

```
1   # in config.yml
2   swiftmailer:
3       delivery_address: %developer_email_address%
4
5   # in parameters.yml
6   parameters:
7       developer_email_address: matthiasnoback@gmail.com
```

But your colleagues may not want to change the default behavior, they just want everything to keep working when they update the project.

10.1 Use local configuration files

The best solution for this problem is to use configuration files which only exist locally. For each environment you can create a local_{env}.yml configuration file. You can then load these local configuration files after loading the original config_{env}.yml files. To accomplish this, modify app/AppKernel.php:

```
1   public function registerContainerConfiguration(LoaderInterface $loader)
2   {
3       $loader->load(__DIR__.'/config/config_'.$this->getEnvironment().'.yml');
4
5       $localFile = __DIR__.'/config/local_'.$this->getEnvironment().'.yml';
6
7       if (is_file($localFile)) {
8           $loader->load($localFile);
9       }
10  }
```

Because the local configuration file will be loaded after the general configuration file, each developer can override any part of the project configuration. When a local configuration file does not exist, the application won't fail to load. This means that deploying your application does not require an extra step.

Don't forget to add the local_{env}.yml files to your .gitignore file. It would also be a good idea to add .dist versions of the local_{env}.yml files, containing some useful suggestions for teammates. Make sure all of these suggestions are commented out:

```
1  # local_dev.yml.dist
2  imports:
3      - { resource: config_dev.yml }
4
5  #swiftmailer:
6  #    delivery_address: your-mail-address@host
```

And also make sure that the `local_{env}.yml.dist` files *will* be committed to your repository.

Keep `parameters.yml`

It would still be a good idea to use parameters for some required configuration values. For example, without a database username and password, your whole application will not work, so it makes sense to ask for these values when installing or updating the project.

If you have a Symfony project with Symfony version less than 2.3, you should install ParameterHandler[1] (create by Incenteev) in your project. From then on, after installing or updating using Composer[2] the ParameterHandler compares the contents of `parameters.yml.dist` with the contents of your current `parameters.yml` and asks you to supply the missing values.

Add a `default_parameters.yml`

Though this configuration setup is becoming pretty flexible already, there are situations where you want to use yet another extra way of configuring things. Consider this MongoDB configuration:

```
1  doctrine_mongodb:
2      connections:
3          default:
4              server: mongodb://%mongo_host%:%mongo_port%
```

You don't want to copy this entire hierarchy to your `local_dev.yml` file to get things up and running on your own machine. You want to be able to use the parameters `%mongo_host%` and `%mongo_port%`. Yet in the default setup of your application these parameters may not vary much. On most developer machines, the host and the port for MongoDB are the same. For this situation, add a `default_parameters.yml`, which contains these parameters, so when making a fresh install of the project, developers don't have to provide these values. Import this file *before* importing `parameters.yml`:

---

[1]https://github.com/Incenteev/ParameterHandler
[2]https://getcomposer.org/

```
1  # in config.yml
2  imports:
3      - { resource: default_parameters.yml }
4      - { resource: parameters.yml }
5
6  # ...
```

In default_parameters.yml you could now add:

```
1  # in default_parameters.yml
2  parameters:
3      mongo_host: localhost
4      mongo_port: 27017
```

And in case your personal MongoDB database is on a different host or port, you can override just these values in parameters.yml:

```
1  # in parameters.yml
2  parameters:
3      mongo_port: 71072
```

When you are using the ParameterHandler mentioned above, in combination with both a default_parameters.yml and a parameters.yml, make sure to add these options to composer.json:

```
1  "extra": {
2      "incenteev-parameters": {
3          "file": "app/config/parameters.yml",
4          "keep-outdated": true
5      }
6  }
```

This way, extra parameters in parameters.yml that override values from default_parameters.yml and are not mentioned in parameters.yml.dist will not be automatically removed from parameters.yml.

 ## In conclusion

Parameters in parameters.yml are essential for a functional application.

Parameters in default_parameters.yml are fallback parameters, you don't **have** to define them in parameters.yml, but you *can* override them.

local_{env}.yml files contain overridden configuration, for your specific situation as a developer.

11 Configuration conventions

Most parts of the application configuration can be loaded from files in many different formats. The application configuration can be provided using plain PHP, Yaml, INI and XML files. The same (except for the INI format) is true for the routing and validation configuration. But these two also add annotations as an option, and so does Doctrine when it comes to entity and document mapping metadata.

You already have the application configuration in order (see the previous chapter), now you have to make choices for your team (maybe settle on this topic together) about the other configuration formats you are going to use in your application.

Make a choice and stick with it

Remember it is less important what you choose (though some formats are more readable or strict than others), it's more important that you stick with your choices and that you enforce this standard in the entire application.

11.1 Routing

Routing as well as template configuration is preferably defined inside the controllers themselves, using annotations:

```
1  use Sensio\Bundle\FrameworkExtraBundle\Configuration\Route;
2  use Sensio\Bundle\FrameworkExtraBundle\Configuration\Method;
3  use Sensio\Bundle\FrameworkExtraBundle\Configuration\Template;
4
5  /**
6   * @Route("/account")
7   */
8  class AccountController
9  {
10     /**
11      * @Route("/new")
12      * @Method({"GET","POST"})
13      * @Template
14      */
15     public function newAction()
16     {
17         return array();
```

```
18        }
19    }
```

Each bundle should have a `Resources/config/routing.yml` file, which loads each controller as a resource:

```
1  MatthiasAccountBundle_AccountController:
2      resource: "@MatthiasAccountBundle/Controller/AccountController.php"
3      type: annotation
4
5  MatthiasAccountBundle_CredentialsController:
6      resource: "@MatthiasAccountBundle/Controller/CredentialsController.php"
7      type: annotation
8
9  # ...
```

Though less explicit, you may also choose to load the routing for an entire controller directory at once:

```
1  MatthiasAccountBundleControllers:
2      resource: "@MatthiasAccountBundle/Controller/"
3      type: annotation
```

The application routing configuration in `/app/config/routing.yml` should have references to the `routing.yml` files of the active bundles:

```
1  MatthiasAccountBundle:
2      resource: "@MatthiasAccountBundle/Resources/config/routing.yml"
```

Choosing Route Names

Route names often become one big mess. We have `account_new`, `account_index`, `accounts`, `account_list`, etc. When an action name changes, the old route name keeps popping up. And when another controller also has a route named `accounts`, it will override the other already existing route, or be overridden itself.

The solution is very simple: follow this pattern (it may sound familiar):

```
1  {name of the bundle without "Bundle"}.{name of the controller without
2  "Controller"}.{name of the action without "Action"}
```

For example, the `AccountController` above has an action `newAction`. The controller is part of the `MatthiasAccountBundle`, so its route name should be `matthias_account.account.new`:

```
1  /**
2   * @Route("/new", name="matthias_account.account.new")
3   */
```

Remember: when you change a route name, make sure you do a project-wide search-and-replace for occurrences of the route name.

11.2 Services

Define your services using XML files. This gives you automatic XML validation, auto-completion and nice syntax highlighting (at least when you are using an IDE which supports this).

```
1  <?xml version="1.0" ?>
2  <container xmlns="http://symfony.com/schema/dic/services"
3            xmlns:xsi="http://www.w3.org/2001/XMLSchema-instance"
4            xsi:schemaLocation="http://symfony.com/schema/dic/services
5            http://symfony.com/schema/dic/services/services-1.0.xsd">
6      <services>
7          <service id="matthias_account.account_controller"
8              class="Matthias\AccountBundle\Controller\AccountController">
9          </service>
10     </services>
11  </container>
```

When choosing ids for services, use only underscores and lowercase characters. Optionally provide namespacing using dots. The service id for the service of class `MailManager` inside the `MatthiasAccountBundle` may be `matthias_account.mail_manager`.

In case your services are divided into several service files, which are all grouped by a common theme (like `metadata`, `form`, etc.), you could insert an extra namespace in the service ids. For instance the service id for the form type of class `CreateAccountType` in the `MatthiasAccountBundle`, defined in the `form.xml` service definition file, may get the id `matthias_account.form.create_account_-type`.

11.3 Mapping metadata

The preferred way of configuring your entities or documents is to use annotations:

```
1  /**
2   * @ORM\Entity
3   * @ORM\Table(name="accounts")
4   */
5  class Account
6  {
7      /**
8       * @ORM\Id
9       * @ORM\Column(type="secure_random_id")
10      */
11     private $id;
12 }
```

When it comes to (potentially) reusable code, you should not use any annotations. Read more about this in Storage-agnostic models.

Recommended conventions

Configure:

- The application in general using Yaml files.
- Routing using annotations and Yaml files.
- Service definitions using XML files.
- Documents and entities using annotations.

V Security

12 Introduction

12.1 Symfony and security

The Symfony Standard Edition comes with the *Security Component*, the *SecurityBundle* and (until version 2.3) the *SecurityExtraBundle*. When configured for your application (using `security.yml`), you can have the following for free:

- One or more secured areas in your application, protected by for instance a login form or HTTP authentication.
- Total freedom in retrieving user data.
- Several ways for hashing user passwords.
- A way to log out.
- Security-related events that are dispatched through the application's event dispatcher.
- Authorization of users based on their roles.
- Configurable session storage handlers (i.e. you can define where session data should be stored).
- Access control list (ACL) functionality, which you can use to assign very specific rights (like edit, view, delete, etc.) to specific users concerning specific objects.

All the things in the list above are all implemented very well, but the many different concepts (like: firewall, authentication listener, authentication provider, exception handler, entry point, ACL, ACE, security identity, object identity, etc.) can lead to much confusion. This is why, when you are building any application in which there is a difference between authenticated users and guest users, or where there are access rights on the object level, you should really read about Security & Symfony. There are some good sources on this subject:

- The chapter Security[1] on symfony.com which gives you the general outline of authentication and authorization management in a Symfony application.
- The documentation for the Security Component[2] (written by myself) describes in more detail all the parts of the component that play a role in securing your application.

The good thing is, there is much to read. Afterwards you should compare Symfony's feature set with your own wish list or ("should list"). Because, the bad thing is that there are also many things missing. Some examples of what's missing or things that you have to create/check yourself:

- Input sanitizing (almost nothing is done automatically for you, so this will be a larger topic later on).

---

[1]http://symfony.com/doc/current/book/security.html

[2]http://symfony.com/doc/current/components/security/index.html

- Automatic (inactivity/time-based) session invalidation.
- Monitoring/preventing session hijacking.
- Preventing brute-force attacks on login forms.
- Storing/managing user types, roles and groups dynamically.
- Showing friendly "access denied" pages.
- Enforcing strong passwords.
- Preventing sensitive information from being cached by browsers.

To be able to judge what should really be done, and exactly which solutions help best to prevent the "evil guys" from spoiling the fun, you should also read about PHP security (server configuration amongst many things) and (web) application security in general. This is a subject about which many people have widely diverging opinions, so after understanding the main problems, you will also need to be able to judge the advice given by many different people. I would like to point out one very good source to you, namely the book-in-progress Survive The Deep End: PHP Security[3], by Pádraic Brady.

When it comes to all the extra security-related measures that are not bundled by default with Symfony, I would like to point you to my own website, where I have posted some articles about security enhancements for your application[4].

 Know your way around in the land of PHP, web application *and* Symfony security. Don't trust "the framework" blindly. And when you have set up your security preventions: know *if* and *why* they work.

12.2 Goals: prevention and confinement

There are two ways in which you can enhance the security of your application: first you can try to prevent a bad thing from happening, second you can make arrangements so that when it happened anyway, things won't get too far out of hand. The OWASP Secure Coding Practices - Quick Reference Guide[5] guide puts this as follows:

> A *threat agent* interacts with a *system*, which may have a *vulnerability* that can be *exploited* in order to cause an *impact*.

Your Symfony application is a *system* which almost certainly has *vulnerabilities* (unless it just displays "Hello world!") and these can be used to break through the thresholds you have placed around your (sensitive) data. Though you should do everything you reasonably can to prevent this from happening, you need to think about what could happen in the case of a security breach. After all, this could be a matter of a leaked password, or even a brute-forced entry to the database server.

---

[3]http://phpsecurity.readthedocs.org/en/latest/

[4]http://php-and-symfony.matthiasnoback.nl/category/security/

[5]https://www.owasp.org/index.php/OWASP_Secure_Coding_Practices_-_Quick_Reference_Guide

What does the "hacker" get, and how much time will it take him to get more? And exactly which data has been compromised? Should you inform users about the attack? Which users? Can you track this down? And in the case of a credentials database, could the hashed passwords be "unhashed" using brute-force tactics in a reasonable amount of time?

For example, when your application has a comment system which allows users to directly write a comment on a page, a malevolent user may try to add a JavaScript snippet to a comment. When you don't have output escaping enabled for these comments, the snippet will just end up on the page as if it were application code. This would be a serious vulnerability of your application. A *threat agent* could inject a piece of JavaScript that examines `document.cookie` to find out the ID of the user's session as it is stored in the session cookie. He may then even hijack the user's session in his own browser.

Minimize impact

The JavaScript injection *exploit* will have quite a big *impact*, since taking over (any) user's sessions is a very dangerous thing, even more so when the user is an administrator. To minimize the impact you should take several security measures. First of all you should configure PHP to mark the session cookie as HTTP-only. This makes it impossible to read from or write to the session cookie in JavaScript. Then you should find a way to detect hijacked sessions and reject them. There are many more options here, and they all reduce the chance of a security breach, but equally important: they also reduce the impact.

Reflection

It is clear that you should try to find and remove vulnerabilities and that you should also minimize the impact of a possible (even an improbable) attack. But what's also important is that you know what you are trying to achieve by a certain security measure. It helps you with determining the right solution, when you know what the problem is that you are trying to solve. Be very reflective about your own ways. Sometimes it will occur to you that you are taking measures that won't help at all, since you already have a stronger security measure in place. And sometimes you will notice that one very insecure part could indirectly give a threat agent access to another, secure part of the system.

Before diving in...

There is so much you can do when it comes to (web) application security - you probably won't be able to implement it all. You also won't need to. Talk with your team members about the necessary security measurements, and some quick wins. But also talk with your manager about the time budget and the importance of security for a specific project (or the organization). Security should be a team effort, and a secure application comes for the biggest part from awareness and discipline. So make sure that everybody on your team thinks alike when it comes to securing the application that you're creating.

In the following chapters I will show you ways in which you can prevent bad things from happening to your Symfony application, but also how you can apply some damage control here and there.

13 Authentication and sessions

As I mentioned earlier, Symfony already takes care of many cases concerning logging in and out, and also has settings for many of the desired behaviors, available in config.yml and security.yml. For instance you can alter some security-related PHP settings directly from within config.yml:

```
1   framework:
2       session:
3           # session cookie name
4           name: matthias_session
5
6           # session cookie should not be accessible using JavaScript
7           cookie_httponly: true
8
9           # session data should expire in n seconds (when not used)
10          gc_maxlifetime: 3600
11
12          # expired session data will be garbage collected with a 1:10 chance
13          gc_probability: 1
14          gc_divisor: 10
```

Symfony takes care of migrating the session (effectively changing the session ID) when you are logging in, to prevent the old, unauthenticated session from getting extra rights (should this session be compromised at any time). Symfony also takes care of invalidating the authenticated session after logging out, to prevent session hijacking. This works just fine by default, but could be configured explicitly in security.yml:

```
1   security:
2       # after authentication, the session will be migrated
3       session_fixation_strategy:  migrate
4
5       firewalls:
6           secured_area:
7               logout:
8                   # the authenticated session will be unavailable afterwards
9                   invalidate_session: true
```

13.1 Invalidating sessions

Session hijacking

All nice and well, but there are some things missing. In the first place, when you would be able to track down the session id of an authenticated user and use it in your own session cookie to take over the authenticated session of a user, no one would notice. You would also not be hindered in your attempt. This means, you have to track changes in the "signature" of the user. For instance, you could check the client's IP address, or his User Agent. Changes in these client characteristics should at the very least be logged, so that you can monitor suspicious behavior. But you may also require a user to re-authenticate and thereby confirm that the changed signature was not intended as a threat to your application.

```
 1  namespace Matthias\SecurityBundle\EventListener;
 2
 3  use Matthias\SecurityBundle\Exception\UserSignatureChangedException;
 4  use Symfony\Component\HttpKernel\Event\GetResponseEvent;
 5  use Symfony\Component\HttpKernel\HttpKernelInterface;
 6
 7  class UserSignatureListener
 8  {
 9      public function onKernelRequest(GetResponseEvent $event)
10      {
11          if ($event->getRequestType()
12                  !== HttpKernelInterface::MASTER_REQUEST) {
13              return;
14          }
15
16          $request = $event->getRequest();
17
18          $clientIp = $request->getClientIp();
19
20          $userAgent = $request->headers->get('user-agent');
21
22          if (...) {
23              throw new UserSignatureChangedException();
24          }
25      }
26  }
```

Using the service definition below, you could register the event listener:

```
1  <service id="matthias_security.user_signature_listener"
2    class="Matthias\SecurityBundle\EventListener\UserSignatureListener">
3      <tag
4        name="kernel.event_listener"
5        event="kernel.request"
6        priority="100"
7        method="onKernelRequest" />
8  </service>
```

The UserSignatureChangedException that will be thrown in the request listener should of course be handled by an exception listener (listen to KernelEvents::EXCEPTION), which sets the appropriate response object, for instance a RedirectResponse to a page where the user can re-authenticate.

Long-running sessions

Say, an authenticated user of your application does nothing for a while, but he keeps the browser open. The session data is not being requested for some time, and its lifetime is almost expired. Then, the user refreshes the page. The session cookie containing the session ID is set only to expire when the browser is closed (cookie_lifetime = 0). The cookie will still be valid, as well as the session data (its lifetime *almost* expired), so the user can continue with his session as if nothing happened. This way there is nothing that prevents a user from having an eternal session.

You may want to invalidate these long-running sessions, based on the date they were last used, or when they were first created. Symfony has no built-in way to do this, but it is very easy to implement some custom session invalidation yourself. The session has a so-called MetadataBag containing Unix timestamps for the time the session was first created and the time its data was last changed.

```
1  use Symfony\Component\HttpKernel\Event\GetResponseEvent;
2  use Symfony\Component\HttpKernel\HttpKernelInterface;
3
4  class SessionAgeListener
5  {
6      public function onKernelRequest(GetResponseEvent $event)
7      {
8          if ($event->getRequestType()
9                  !== HttpKernelInterface::MASTER_REQUEST) {
10             return;
11         }
12
13         $session = $event->getRequest()->getSession();
14         $metadataBag = $session->getMetadataBag();
15
16         $lastUsed = $metadataBag->getLastUsed();
17         if ($lastUsed === null) {
```

```
18              // the session was created just now
19              return;
20          }
21
22          $createdAt = $metadataBag->getCreated();
23
24          $now = time();
25
26          // $now, $lastUsed and $createdAt are Unix timestamps
27
28          // if a session is being revived after too many seconds:
29          $session->invalidate();
30
31          // create some nice response to let the user know this happened:
32          $event->setResponse(...);
33      }
34  }
```

The service definition below activates the SessionAgeListener:

```
1  <service id="matthias_security.verify_session_listener"
2    class="Matthias\SecurityBundle\EventListener\SessionAgeListener">
3      <tag
4          name="kernel.event_listener"
5          event="kernel.request"
6          priority="100"
7          method="onKernelRequest" />
8  </service>
```

Logging security-related information

Whenever something odd happens (the user suddenly has a different IP address, a user has tried to log in with the wrong credentials 100 times during the last minute, etc.), you should write something to the application's log file. It should be recognizable that the problem is related to security. To get the appropriate logger service, tag your service using the monolog.logger tag:

```
1  <service id="matthias_security.verify_session_listener"
2      class="...">
3      <argument type="service" id="logger" on-invalid="null" />
4      <tag name="monolog.logger" channel="security" />
5  </service>
```

Whenever you use the injected logger service:

```
1  $this->logger->warning('Old session reused')
```

You will see something like this in your log file:

```
1  [2013-07-06 16:35:45] security.WARNING: Old session reused
```

14 Controller design

When it comes to controller design, I recommend creating small controller classes. First of all this means grouping logically related actions together in one controller class, but also creating only small actions, with no real logic inside and at most two possible execution paths. This may mean that you end up with many controllers, but this method has many advantages, which are also related to security:

1. When you need to change some user-related behavior, you can very quickly find your way from URL, to route name, to controller.
2. When some controllers need special attention from a security point of view, you can easily spot them and concentrate the protection logic in one place.

To illustrate the second point, let's say you have one controller concerned with personal settings, but it relates to data like strictly personal account information, payment information like a credit card number and public profile data, like a nickname or an avatar. I would recommend splitting the pages concerned with viewing and editing this data over multiple controllers, each with a simple and recognizable name. Inside the controllers, each action should also have a recognizable name, which can be longer than you think, like `AccountController::editAccountInformation` (instead of just "edit") and `PaymentController::listCreditCards`. This allows you to align your personal alertness level with the level required by the specific code you are going to work on.

Furthermore it should be clear by looking at the code, which controllers are used for modifying the state of the application, i.e. persist or remove some data. You should explicitly define the HTTP methods allowed for a given action. In this sense, pages that can be requested using the GET method are innocent, and pages to which users can POST data, are not.

```
1   use Sensio\Bundle\FrameworkExtraBundle\Configuration\Method;
2
3   /**
4    * @Method("GET")
5    */
6   public function viewPublicProfileAction()
7   {
8   }
9
10  /**
11   * @Method("GET")
12   */
13  public function editPublicProfileAction()
14  {
```

```
15  }
16
17  /**
18   * @Method("POST")
19   */
20  public function updatePublicProfileAction()
21  {
22  }
```

Of course, it is already bad when someone can view an edit form without the given object being an object he can modify, but it is worse if he can do real modifications to the object.

14.1 Secure actions

There are many ways in which you can secure actions. The action code itself will sometimes throw an AccessDeniedException, and of course, you should check that a certain object belongs to someone, or can be modified by someone (either because the owner is stored as a property of an object, or because the correct rights are registered using ACL). But you should also implement role management in some way. Roles are very cheap when using Symfony. Just think of a new one and it already exists. When existing roles should include the new role, add it to the "role hierarchy" as defined in security.yml.

It is very important to start adding a list of roles for any controller which requires a user to be logged in. There are some good reasons for this. First of all, when it comes to security you should adhere to the principle of "least privilege". This means that by default an authenticated user can do nothing at all (maybe only change his password). You, the system, or an administrator will have to give him extra rights first. You can use all kinds of expressions concerning roles above an action, using the @PreAuthorize annotation, but in most situations I have encountered, a simple @Secure suffices:

```
1  use JMS\SecurityExtraBundle\Annotation\Secure;
2
3  /**
4   * @Secure("ROLE_PAGE_EDITOR")
5   */
6  public function editPageAction()
7  {
8  }
```

Often there are different types of users who should have access to this editPageAction, for instance a user with ROLE_ADMINISTRATOR but also someone with ROLE_CONTENT_MANAGER. The solution here is not to add extra roles to the @Secure annotation (like @Secure({"ROLE_ADMINISTRATOR", "ROLE_CONTENT_MANAGER"})) but to solve this by changing the role hierarchy:

```
1  security:
2    role_hierarchy:
3      ROLE_ADMINISTRATOR: [ROLE_PAGE_EDITOR]
4      ROLE_CONTENT_MANAGER: [ROLE_PAGE_EDITOR]
```

When it comes to roles, remember:

- Roles are volatile: you are free to create and almost free to remove them (basically they are just strings)
- It works best when a role describes the user having the role (role names ideally end with "MANAGER", "EDITOR", "MODERATOR", etc.)

14.2 Putting controllers behind the firewall

Now that you have many controllers all inside something like a SettingsBundle, you should import them all in this bundle's routing.yml file:

```
1  SettingsBundleControllers:
2    resource: "@SettingsBundle/Controller/"
3    type: annotation
```

This entire file can be imported at once from the applications' routing.yml file. This enables you to define a prefix for all routes in the SettingsBundle together:

```
1  SettingsBundle:
2    resource: "@SettingsBundle/Resources/config/routing.yml"
3    type: yaml
4    prefix: /settings
```

Using this prefix, you can easily define a set of required roles for any URI starting with /settings:

```
1  security:
2    access_control:
3      - { path: ^/settings, roles: [IS_AUTHENTICATED_FULLY] }
```

The line above means that you need to be fully authenticated to do anything on settings-related pages (when you are logged in just by a "remember me" cookie, this would not suffice to grant you access). This is a good thing, and you now also have a single point of control for this security measure.

15 Input validation

Any input your application receives from the outside world should be checked and processed before actually being used or stored in any way.

15.1 Safe forms

Symfony has several important tools that you can use in the fight for clean input: the Form Component and the Validator Component. Most Symfony developers already trust the Form Component with their lives:

```
1  if ($request->isMethod('POST')) {
2      $form->bind($request);
3      if ($form->isValid()) {
4          // persist!
5      }
6  }
```

This is mostly a good thing since the Form and Validator Component both are quite good, and they can be trusted to do what they say. But: you should not trust them blindly (what *can* you trust blindly?).

HTML5 validation

Back in the days when we used to write PHP applications by hand from start to end, we were taught to validate form input. For instance we did not want users to leave the "name" field blank. But now we can build a form in a form (which represents the field) and we set it's `required` option to `true`. When you open the form in the browser and try to submit it with no values inserted, it will show you a nice error message (which is in fact a feature of HTML5) instead of immediately submitting the form. However, if you disable this client-side validation, by adding a `novalidate` HTML5 attribute to the `form` tag, you will notice that by default there is no server-side validation at all. So, the first thing you need to do when working with forms (and maybe for the `dev` environment only) is disabling the HTML5 validation:

```
1  <form{% if app.debug %} novalidate="true"{% endif %}>
```

Now you can test the server-side validation of your form.

Validation constraints

Usually you have some domain object, let's say an entity, that you want to create or modify using a form. You would then set the form's `data_class` option to the class name of this entity. In the `buildForm` method you can instruct the `FormBuilder` to add certain fields corresponding to attributes of the entity. Now to validate the form data, you need to be very secure in adding constraints to the attributes (in my opinion preferably using annotations). This is nothing but the usual, and it's very well documented[1]:

```
1   namespace Matthias\AccountBundle\Entity;
2
3   use Symfony\Component\Validator\Constraints as Assert;
4
5   class User
6   {
7       /**
8        * @Assert\Email()
9        * @Assert\NotBlank()
10       */
11      private $emailAddress;
12  }
```

Custom validation constraints

There are times where the standard validation constraints bundled with the Symfony Validator Component are not (specific) enough for validating your data. Don't give up and add custom validation constraints[2], and custom validators for validating this data.

Forms without an entity

When you have data which does not have a one-to-one correspondence to an entity, the Forms documentation tells you that you can just provide *no data class* and in fact build the form inline inside your controller:

---

[1] http://symfony.com/doc/master/book/forms.html
[2] http://symfony.com/doc/current/cookbook/validation/custom_constraint.html

```
 1  public function contactAction(Request $request)
 2  {
 3      $defaultData = array('message' => 'Type your message here');
 4      $form = $this->createFormBuilder($defaultData)
 5          ->add('name', 'text')
 6          ->add('email', 'email')
 7          ->add('message', 'textarea')
 8          ->getForm();
 9
10      $form->handleRequest($request);
11
12      if ($form->isValid()) {
13          // data is an array with "name", "email", and "message" keys
14          $data = $form->getData();
15      }
16  }
```

This to me sounds like a bad idea, for two reasons: first of all, you should always define a form using a custom form type (extending from AbstractType), like this:

```
 1  use Symfony\Component\Form\AbstractType;
 2  use Symfony\Component\Form\FormBuilderInterface;
 3
 4  class ContactFormType extends AbstractType
 5  {
 6      public function buildForm(
 7          FormBuilderInterface $builder,
 8          array $options
 9      ) {
10          $builder
11              ->add('name', 'text')
12              ->add('email', 'email')
13              ->add('message', 'textarea')
14          ;
15      }
16
17      public function getName()
18      {
19          return 'contact_form';
20      }
21  }
```

This will put all the logic related to the form in one place, making it reusable and much better maintainable.

But you should also always provide a `data_class` option. The data from the contact form will not be persisted, but still it has a certain coherent structure and also a very clear meaning. So choose a suitable name for the data object of your form, like `ContactDetails`, create a class with the right fields and add some assertions to each field to ensure the object contains consistent data:

```
1  use Symfony\Component\Validator\Constraints as Assert;
2
3  class ContactDetails
4  {
5      /**
6       * @Assert\NotBlank
7       */
8      private $name;
9
10     /**
11      * @Assert\NotBlank
12      * @Assert\Email
13      */
14     private $email;
15
16     /**
17      * @Assert\NotBlank
18      */
19     private $message;
20
21     // add getters and setters for all fields
22 }
```

Now set this class as the `data_class` option of the `ContactFormType`:

```
1  use Symfony\Component\OptionsResolver\OptionsResolverInterface;
2
3  class ContactFormType extends AbstractType
4  {
5      public function setDefaultOptions(OptionsResolverInterface $resolver)
6      {
7          $resolver->setDefaults(array(
8              'data_class' => 'LifeOnline\ContactBundle\Model\ContactDetails'
9          ));
10     }
11 }
```

Your data will be in much better shape since it is now encapsulated, validated and totally under control. You can:

- Prevent bad data from entering the attributes by filtering the data in setters:

```
1    class ContactDetails
2    {
3        public function setMessage($message)
4        {
5            $this->message = strip_tags($message);
6        }
7    }
```

- Provide default values a lot easier (without having to know the structure of the expected array):

```
1    public function contactAction(Request $request)
2    {
3        $contactDetails = ContactDetails::createForUser($this->getUser());
4
5        $form = $this->createForm(new ContactFormType(), $contactDetails);
6
7        // ...
8    }
```

- Work with an object of a known type, after binding and validating the form:

```
1    public function contactAction(Request $request)
2    {
3        $form = $this->createForm(new ContactFormType());
4
5        if ($request->isMethod('POST')) {
6            $form->bind($request);
7            if ($form->isValid()) {
8                $contactDetails = $form->getData();
9
10               // $contactDetails is an instance of ContactDetails
11           }
12       }
13   }
```

All forms in your application should...

- Have a data_class option pointing to a specific class.
- Be defined in their own class extending from AbstractType.
- Preferably have their own service definition, for better reusability.

15.2 Validate values from Request

The Request object is in part just a wrapper for PHP's superglobals. In /web/app.php you can see how the Request object gets created:

```
1   $request = Request::createFromGlobals();
```

Inside this method you find this simple line of code:

```
1   $request = new static($_GET, $_POST, array(), $_COOKIE, $_FILES, $_SERVER);
```

So even though it may feel much more secure to fetch request data using

```
1   $request->query->get('page')
```

it is in fact no more secure than just $_GET['page']. Though within the Symfony context it is always better to use the methods on the Request class, you should still be wary about these values, validate them and force them into the right format. Strict typing, and checking for allowed values and ranges is quite necessary.

Request attributes

Route parameters

First of all, when a URI pattern contains wildcard values, like id in /comment/{id}, and a certain request matches this pattern, the RouterListener will make sure that all the parameters are copied over to the request object as attributes. These request attributes will be used by the ControllerResolver to collect arguments for the controller based on its parameter names and type hints. See Events leading to a response for a more detailed explanation of this process.

Since most controller arguments are being copied more or less directly from the URI of the request, you need to be extra careful when it comes to handling them. First of all you have to think about requirements for route parameters (like id). Requirements are to be defined as regular expressions. The default requirement for route parameters is [^/]+: they may contain any character except a slash. So you must always define your own requirements, like \w+, which means at least one "word" character (i.e. a-z, A-Z or 0-9, or underscore) or \d+, which means at least one "number" character (i.e. 0-9). If you don't know regular expressions yet, you should really learn them (as you may have noticed they are also used when working with paths defined in security.yml). Below you will find some examples of route parameters with requirements:

```
1   /**
2    * id can only be a number:
3    * @Route("/comment/{id}", requirements={"id"="\d+"})
4    */
5
6   /**
7    * alias can be at least one lowercase letter, a number or a dash:
8    * @Route("/user/{alias}", requirements={"alias"="[a-z0-9\-]+"})
9    */
10
11  /**
12   * type can only be commercial or non-commercial:
13   * @Route("/create-account/{type}", requirements={
14   *    "type"="commercial|non-commercial"
15   * })
16   */
```

It is important to verify the correctness of these values in this early stage, otherwise incorrect values might result as arguments of method calls to services, where they may cause InvalidArgumentExceptions, or worse: unexplainable errors.

Query or request parameters

There are also situations where you want to be more flexible concerning the input for your controller: you may want to support query parameters in your URI, like ?page=1, or request parameters sent using the content of the request (e.g. POST data). But these values are by no means trustworthy. Query and POST data can both easily be modified to *not* be what you expect it to be. Therefore, when you retrieve this data from the Request object:

- Let validation be handled by the Form and Validator Component by using Form::bind() and Form::isValid()
- Or:
    - Cast the values to the type that you expect (in most situations either a string or an integer) and
    - Validate these values yourself by calling the validateValue() method of the validator service. You could think of validating the range of a value ("should be at least 1"), or one of multiple options ("should be any of 'commercial', 'non-commercial'").

For instance:

```
1   use Symfony\Component\Validator\Constraints\Choice;
2
3   public function createAccountAction()
4   {
5       $userTypeConstraint = new Choice(array(
6           'choices' => array('commercial', 'non-commercial')
7       );
8
9       $errorList = $this->get('validator')->validateValue(
10          $request->query->get('userType'),
11          $userTypeConstraint
12      );
13
14      if (count($errorList) == 0) {
15          // the provided user type is valid
16      }
17  }
```

Don't use `$request->get()`

Don't use `$request->get()`, because this is what happens inside:

```
1   public function get($key, $default = null, $deep = false)
2   {
3       return $this->query->get($key,
4           $this->attributes->get($key,
5               $this->request->get($key, $default, $deep),
6           $deep),
7       $deep);
8   }
```

Always retrieve values specifically from the query, the request data or the request attributes. When you are used to using PHP superglobals, this is the translation to the respective parameter bags of the Request class:

`$_GET['key']` ⇒ "$request->query->get('key')

`$_POST['key']` ⇒ "$request->request->get('key')

Use the ParamFetcher

There is one tool that I would like to mention here. It is part of the FOSRestBundle[3] which provides many tools for easily creating a REST-like webservice. It provides a very nice way of pre-validating

---

[3]https://github.com/FriendsOfSymfony/FOSRestBundle

query parameters by first adding some configuration in the form of an annotation for each query parameter that you need. For example, this is how you can configure a page query parameter which should consist only of digits, being "1" by default:

```
1   use FOS\RestBundle\Request\ParamFetcher;
2   use FOS\RestBundle\Controller\Annotations\QueryParam;
3
4   /**
5    * @QueryParam(
6    *   name="page",
7    *   requirements="\d+",
8    *   default="1",
9    *   description="Page number"
10   * )
11   */
12  public function listAction(ParamFetcher $paramFetcher)
13  {
14      $page = $paramFetcher->get('page');
15  }
```

It works almost exactly the same for POST data without a corresponding form:

```
1   use FOS\RestBundle\Request\ParamFetcher;
2   use FOS\RestBundle\Controller\Annotations\RequestParam;
3
4   /**
5    * @RequestParam(name="username", requirements="\w+")
6    */
7   public function deleteAccountAction(ParamFetcher $paramFetcher)
8   {
9       ...
10  }
```

Even though your application will not have a REST API, you can still just install the FOSRest-Bundle bundle without many side-effects. Just make sure you disable all built-in listeners except the ParamFetcherListener:

```
1   # in /app/config/config.yml
2   fos_rest:
3       param_fetcher_listener: true
```

15.3 Sanitizing HTML

You likely have forms in your application allowing users to enter some kind of rich text, with bold, italic or underlined text, and maybe you allow users to add their own link tags. Well, this is of course a very dangerous thing when it comes to security. You should take very good care of restricting users in their use of HTML tags but also in them adding HTML attributes, which can actually be more dangerous, especially when they contain JavaScript. And don't think that `alert('Hi!');` is the worst thing a user can do. Even mismatching tags can spoil things - think about what a simple `</div>` in some random spot could do in most sites.

First of all: don't rely on things like Markdown to solve your HTML injection problem. The specification of Markdown clearly says that any HTML in the source text should be left intact and added "as is" to the generated output. Second: don't rely on the second argument of `strip_tags` to allow some tags since this also allows *any* attribute for these tags. Third: don't dream up your own regular expressions for allowing some tags and attributes. There will always be hacks that circumvent your handwritten rules. Instead, use HTMLPurifier[4] and configure it properly for specific situations allowing rich (HTML) text.

There is an excellent bundle which integrates HTMLPurifier with any Symfony application: the ExerciseHTMLPurifierBundle[5]. It defines HTMLPurifier services for each configuration set you define in `config.yml`. It also supports automatic filtering of form values.

Automatic sanitizing

The thing is: with every Symfony application you have to manually take care of sanitizing input. It would be great if all request attributes would be automatically filtered according to some rules, or when every form or entity would contain only known-to-be-clean values. Unfortunately there is no such thing in the open source world that I am aware of right now. A prototype of the desired functionality can be found in the DMSFilterBundle[6], but in its current state this bundle does not handle every situation well. It filters only form input for the root objects of forms. It also does not filter values manually set upon entities, documents, etc.

---

[4] http://htmlpurifier.org/

[5] https://github.com/Exercise/HTMLPurifierBundle

[6] https://github.com/rdohms/DMSFilterBundle

16 Output escaping

16.1 Twig

Symfony developers are told that:

> If you're using Twig, output escaping is on by default and you're protected.

Everyone will be very happy after reading this, except a security-minded person, who is very skeptical about remarks like this. There is no such thing as automatic output escaping that works in all situations. The default output escaping for Symfony assumes that you are rendering in an HTML context, at the element level. Also Twig follows many special (though secure rules) for auto-escaping, which you should know about. Read about all of them in the Twig documentation for developers[1].

Know your escaping context

Most important is this assumption about the default context being html. This will likely not be the only context in your application. You need to find out which variables are being printed where and in what context. Twig supports these contexts out of the box:

html
> When rendering variables at the HTML element level

html_attr
> When rendering variables inside HTML attributes

js   When rendering variables inside JavaScript code

css   When rendering variables inside a stylesheet

url   When rendering a part of a URL (like a query parameter)

When you have determined the context and it is something other than html, escape as appropriate using the Twig escape filter:

```
1  {{ someVariable|escape('js') }}
```

Escaping function output

You always have to be at guard when it comes to auto-escaping. Especially when you create your own Twig functions, (or filters). The output of your functions will also be automatically escaped in the current context (usually html):

---

[1]http://twig.sensiolabs.org/doc/api.html#escaper-extension

```
1  class MyTwigExtension extends \Twig_Extension
2  {
3      public function getFunctions()
4      {
5          return array(
6              \Twig_SimpleFunction('important', function($thing) {
7                  return sprintf(
8                      '<strong>%s</strong> is important to me',
9                      $thing
10                 );
11             })
12         );
13     }
14 }
```

The result of this function will be auto-escaped, so:

```
1  {{ important('My family') }}
```

Will result in:

```
1  &lt;strong&gt;My family&lt;/strong&gt; is important to me
```

Except when you add an `is_safe` option when defining the function in your Twig extension:

```
1  class MyTwigExtension extends \Twig_Extension
2  {
3      public function getFunctions()
4      {
5          return array(
6              \Twig_SimpleFunction('important', function($thing) {
7                  ...
8              }, array(
9                  'is_safe' => array('html')
10             )
11         );
12     }
13 }
```

Now, the output will not be escaped. *But, so will the input!*

Escaping function arguments

When we have marked the output of a function as safe but we nevertheless include function arguments in this same output, we end up with a totally unsafe function. So:

```
1   {{ important('<script>alert("Security")</script>') }}
```

Will result in:

```
1   <strong><script>alert("Security")</script></strong> is important to me
```

Now of course you would not type such a thing in your own templates like this, but most of the time you just pass some user-supplied value as an argument to Twig functions (and remember that even most of the things in your database originate from user input). And such a value can be anything, assuming it may not have been correctly sanitized.

Well, there is an easy solution: add a pre_escape option:

```
1   class MyTwigExtension extends \Twig_Extension
2   {
3       public function getFunctions()
4       {
5           return array(
6               \Twig_SimpleFunction('important', function($thing) {
7                   ...
8               }, array(
9                   'is_safe' => array('html'),
10                  'pre_escape' => 'html'
11              )
12          );
13      }
14  }
```

Now all arguments provided to the function will first be escaped for the given context.

Be wary of the `raw` filter

You can override any auto-escaping functionality by ending an expression with the raw filter:

```
1   {{ message|raw }}
```

This would escape nothing, and when the message variable contains some HTML, it will be left as-is. This means that you have to be sure that everything has been done to prevent bad things from happening. Which in most cases means: you must be sure that this variable has gone through some kind of sanitizing process (like purifying it using HTMLPurifier, see above). Or (and preferably *and*) that the source of the value can be trusted - for example an imported piece of source code, written by a developer. Not, however, the value of a textarea field submitted by an "administrator". If the security of your authentication system has by any means be compromised, someone may enter some very malevolent text in that specific field and immediately affect many users of your application. I am not saying that you should be scared, but rather cautious.

Twig security scan

Regularly scan the Twig functions and filters used in your project for the use of `is_safe` and missing `pre_escape` options. Also verify that every variable with a `raw` filter originates from a trusted source.

17 Being secretive

In many cases hacking a system means getting to know as much as possible about its inner workings, to know what its sensitive and thus exploitable parts are. Therefore you need to be careful about what you display to outsiders.

17.1 Mask authentication errors

The Symfony documentation shows a very bad example of application security, where literal exception messages are shown above an authentication form (error is an Exception object):

```
1  {% if error %}
2      <div>{{ error.message }}</div>
3  {% endif %}
```

Directly afterwards we are encouraged to "use the exception message wisely", since it may contain sensitive information. It definitely will, as I have noticed on many occasions. Sometimes even raw database errors, including entire schema definitions can end up in the template when you display the exception message directly.

Luckily all exceptions that extend from AuthenticationException have a method getMessageKey. When calling this method you get a cleaner exception message, with no (sensitive) details about the exceptional situation itself. Just simple messages like "Invalid credentials." or "Authentication request could not be processed due to a system problem.".

So the correct Twig template around a login form would display errors like this:

```
1  {% if error %}
2      <div>{{ error.messageKey }}</div>
3  {% endif %}
```

17.2 Prevent exceptions from showing up

When there are places in your application where you want to use exceptions for showing an error message to the user, there are three possible strategies. Either use something like described above (using a getMessageKey() method, which contains a message that is more user-friendly and also more vague) or wrap lower-level exceptions in more high-level, general exceptions and set a new message that is safe for display. You should also be wary of general exceptions occurring at deeper levels of abstraction, which you mistakenly take for one of your own exceptions. You might also mark some exceptions as safe, by filtering them:

```
1   $error = null;
2
3   try {
4       // do something dangerous
5       ...
6   } catch (SomeSpecificException $exception) {
7       $error = $exception;
8   } catch (\Exception $previous) {
9       // unexpected, and unknown exception
10      $error = new GenericException('An error occurred', null, $previous);
11  }
12
13  // $error can be safely used now
```

The problem with this approach is that Symfony's default exception handler (which also logs exceptions when logging is enabled) will not be notified of the truly unexpected exception. As it is most likely a symptom of some problem on a deeper level of the application code, this may not be desired behavior. Therefore, in most situations it suffices to catch specific, known exceptions and let any other exception just bubble up.

17.3 Customize error pages

When such a "normal" exception, indicating a system failure, bubbles up to the standard exception handler, you must be sure to prevent anything from being displayed in the response to the user. Any system information leaked to a user may be used to determine a strategy for compromising the system. You should therefore create custom error pages[1] which blend in well with the rest of your application. Never show any generated information about the problem, especially no stack trace. Problems will be logged automatically and can also be sent to you by email, either by configuring Monolog to do so[2], or by using some other logging tool which sends you alerts when something goes wrong. The latter may be a better choice, since maybe the application has become so unstable that it can not be trusted to do so itself.

17.4 Be vague about user data

Authentication problems are mostly covered by the Symfony Security Component. There are however many bad interaction design decisions that may accidentally disclose sensitive information about users of your system. When your system leaks information about which other users there are, your system is susceptible to something called "harvesting". These are some examples of interaction design that leak information about users.

---

[1]http://symfony.com/doc/master/cookbook/controller/error_pages.html

[2]http://symfony.com/doc/master/cookbook/logging/monolog_email.html

1. A user can reset his password on the "Forgot password" page which contains an "Email" text field. When the user provides his email address and submits the form, the system finds the account record of the corresponding user and generates a "password reset link", then sends a mail to the user containing this link. After submitting the form, the page says: "We have sent a password reset mail to the given email address".

    The problem is: when someone tries to collect email addresses of users, he will now know that a user with the provided email address actually exists in the system.

2. Same situation as above, but now the message is: "If the provided email address belongs to one of our users, we have sent a password reset mail to it."

    This seems secure, however: the request duration is notably longer when an email address is of a known user of the system, than when the email address is unknown. Someone who is harvesting user email addresses may infer based on the length of the request whether an email address is known or unknown to the system. This is called a *timing attack*.

3. When the user is logged in he is allowed to change his email address using a simple form with one field: "Email". After submitting the form the system changes the user's email address or it shows a message to the user saying: "The provided email address is already in use".

    Again: we now know the email address of a user, even though this is sensitive data.

The best solution to prevent harvesting is to be vague: don't say if there was a match, if you have sent an email, etc. You also have to make sure that it can not be guessed if any of these things has been done by measuring the duration of the request.

The solution to the third problem would be:

1. Allow the user to change his email address, but don't persist the change immediately.
2. Send an email to the new address, with a link allowing the user to confirm the requested change.
3. After confirming the change, update the account information with the new email address.

VI Using annotations

18 Introduction

The first release of Symfony2 came bundled with the Doctrine Common library[1]. This library contains some tools used by all the second-generation Doctrine projects, like the Doctrine ORM, Doctrine MongoDB ODM, etc. The library offers shared functionality and utility classes, like an event manager, persistence- related interfaces, some useful base classes and: an *annotation reader.*

The annotation reader was initially only used by Doctrine ORM to parse annotations inside entity classes. Doctrine ORM (or Doctrine2) introduced annotations as a way to specify how a simple PHP class should be mapped to a relational database table:

```
1   use Doctrine\ORM\Mapping as ORM;
2
3   /**
4    * @ORM\Entity
5    */
6   class User
7   {
8       /**
9        * @ORM\Column(type="string")
10       */
11      private $name;
12  }
```

This "syntactic sugar" was soon recognized to be a really useful alternative for the existing solutions, like writing down your mapping configuration in a Yaml or XML file. The creators of Symfony2 also embraced annotations and started adding them to their components as an alternative way of loading configuration. For instance, the Validator component supports annotations to configure validation rules for classes. And the Routing component has annotations for linking a route to a class and one of its methods.

Annotations: Domain-specific languages

Annotations have some very interesting characteristics. They are not written in the PHP language: `@Route("/admin/", name="admin_index")` can not be parsed by the PHP interpreter. Nevertheless, annotations have a "runtime" aspect, since they are parsed by an annotation reader *from within* a running PHP application. Their mere presence has some very real effects on the way the application runs.

Furthermore, annotations are easy to write. Once you know all the attributes an annotation supports, you know all there is to using it in your application. The funny

---

[1] http://docs.doctrine-project.org/projects/doctrine-common/en/latest/

thing is: you don't even need to be a PHP programmer to use an annotation, since you are not required to write any PHP code.

Finally, annotations are always domain-specific. They are introduced as a means to convey some high-level concept from a specific domain, like routing, templating, persistence, etc. Annotations help you abstract from the details and instead think in higher-level concepts.

These characteristics add up to the following conclusion: we should consider annotations as a form of domain-specific languages (DSL)[2]. A DSL is a small language that is used to convert higher-level concepts into lower-level details. It is implemented in a general purpose language like PHP, but can have its own syntax (in this case "annotation syntax").

Each domain specific set of annotations forms a domain-specific language to express the details underlying the high-level domain concepts. For example, the annotations provided by Doctrine ORM form a little language to express inside an entity class at a high level what should happen inside the relational database at a low level to make it ready for storing entities in it. This means that when you use Doctrine annotations to configure the mapping for an entity, you don't have to worry about implementation details like: what is the best way to define a boolean column, or what was the syntax for making a column's value "required" again?

When I first started to work with Symfony2 I saw everyone using annotations. I felt some hesitation to use them too. It seemed to me quite dangerous to use comments to influence the flow of an application. Then after a couple of months I got used to working with annotations and as it happens I never encountered a "dangerous situation" caused by an annotation after all.

Instead, I learned more about annotations: what they really are and how they are used by Symfony, Doctrine, etc. Soon I started creating my own annotations and using them for many different purposes inside the Symfony applications I've been working on. In this chapter I'd like to share my findings with you. You will learn about the inner workings of annotations and how to create them yourself. In the last chapter of this part I show you some Symfony-specific ways in which you can use annotations to influence the application's flow.

---

[2]http://martinfowler.com/books/dsl.html

19 An annotation is a simple value object

You will always find annotations inside so-called doc blocks, which are basically comments but they start with /**. Regular annotations start with @ and serve as documentation for the code that immediately follows it, like this:

```
1   /**
2    * @param int $id The ID of the user
3    * @return array  Template variables
4    */
5   public function editAction($id)
6   {
7       ...
8   }
```

When parsing a doc block, the Doctrine annotation reader will skip all regular annotations, like @param and @return, based on a pre-configured list. When an annotation is not on that list, the annotation reader will assume that the annotation is a class name. For example, the @Route annotation of the UserController::editAction() in the code sample below is actually a class name: Sensio\Bundle\FrameworkExtraBundle\Configuration\Route, which has been imported by the use statement:

```
1   use Sensio\Bundle\FrameworkExtraBundle\Configuration\Route;
2
3   class UserController
4   {
5       /**
6        * @Route("/users/{id}/edit", name="user.edit")
7        */
8       public function editAction($id)
9       {
10          ...
11      }
12  }
```

The annotation reader will try to create an instance of that class and fill it with the data between the brackets ("/users/{id}/edit", name="user.edit"). The resulting Route object can then be used by the routing loader to add an extra route to the RouteCollection.

In every Symfony application an instance of the Doctrine annotation reader is already available as the annotation_reader service:

```
1   // get the service container
2   $container = ...
3
4   $reader = $container->get('annotation_reader');
```

To parse the doc block of the `UserController::editAction()` we need to create a reflection object[1] for that method first:

```
1   $method = new \ReflectionMethod('UserController', 'editAction');
```

Then we can ask the annotation reader to parse the annotations of the reflected method:

```
1   $annotations = $reader->getMethodAnnotations($method);
```

The result of parsing the method annotations would be an array with one `Route` object. The object properties contain the attributes that were provided with the `@Route` annotation:

```
1   print_r($annotations);
2
3   /*
4   Array
5   (
6       [0] => Sensio\Bundle\FrameworkExtraBundle\Configuration\Route Object
7           (
8               ...
9               [path]
10                  => /users/{id}/edit
11              [name]
12                  => user.edit
13              ...
14          )
15  )
16  */
```

Each annotation class (like the `Route` class) needs to have an `@Annotation` annotation itself in order to be recognized by the annotation reader as a valid annotation:

---

[1]http://php.net/manual/en/intro.reflection.php

```
1   /**
2    * @Annotation
3    */
4   class MyAnnotation
5   {
6   }
```

With the @Annotation annotation in place, the MyAnnotation class can be used as a real annotation for a class, a method or a property:

```
1   /**
2    * @MyAnnotation
3    */
4   class SomeClass
5   {
6       /**
7        * @MyAnnotation
8        */
9       private $someProperty;
10
11      /**
12       * @MyAnnotation
13       */
14      public function someFunction()
15      {
16      }
17
18      /**
19       * @MyAnnotation(@MyAnnotation)
20       */
21      public function otherFunction()
22      {
23      }
24  }
```

It is even possible to use @MyAnnotation inside another @MyAnnotation, as you can see inside the doc block of SomeClass::otherFunction().

When we ask the annotation reader to parse the class annotations for SomeClass, it will return an array with one object: an instance of MyAnnotation:

```
1   // get the annotation reader
2   $reader = ...
3
4   $class = new \ReflectionClass('SomeClass');
5   $annotations = $reader->getClassAnnotations($class);
6
7   print_r($annotations);
8
9   /*
10  Array(
11      [0] => MyAnnotation object
12  )
13  */
```

19.1 Adding attributes to your annotation

To be able to define your own annotations is already very nice, but they become more useful when you store some data inside them. This data can be provided by the user when they add your annotation to one of their classes, methods, etc.

The annotation parser supports many different kinds of syntaxes for populating the attributes of an annotation. It accepts strings, numbers, boolean values, arrays and objects (which are themselves annotations). For example:

```
1   /**
2    * @MyAnnotation(
3    *     "some string",
4    *     "hashMap" = {
5    *         "key" = "value"
6    *     },
7    *     "booleanValue" = true,
8    *     "nestedAnnotation" = @MyAnnotation
9    * )
10   */
```

Any logical combination of types is possible. For instance, it's possible to put each scalar or object type inside a hash map.

When the user has provided some data for the annotation, like in the example above, the annotation reader needs to pass that data to the annotation object it creates. There are two different strategies which the annotation parser can apply.

Passing the attributes via the constructor

First, the annotation parser will look inside the MyAnnotation class for the presence of a constructor. If it finds one, it passes all the attributes as the first argument of the constructor when it creates an instance of the MyAnnotation class:

```
1   /**
2    * @Annotation
3    */
4   class MyAnnotation
5   {
6       public function __construct(array $attributes)
7       {
8           // "some string"
9           $value = $attributes['value'];
10
11          // array('key' => 'value', ...)
12          $hashMap = $attributes['hashMap'];
13
14          // true
15          $booleanValue = $attributes['booleanValue'];
16
17          // an instance of MyAnnotation
18          $nestedAnnotation = $attributes['nestedAnnotation'];
19      }
20  }
```

From then on you can do anything you like with those values. You would probably validate them and store them in private properties.

Populating public properties with the provided attributes

If there is no constructor (or the constructor has no first argument), the parser will try to copy the attributes that were provided into public properties of the MyAnnotation class:

```
1   /**
2    * @Annotation
3    */
4   class MyAnnotation
5   {
6       public $value;
7       public $hashMap;
8       public $booleanValue;
9       public $nestedAnnotation;
10  }
```

Using this second strategy you have no chance to validate the attributes before they are copied into the public properties. Luckily it is possible to add some basic validation rules directly inside the annotation class itself.

Validation using `@Attributes`

We can add an `@Attributes` annotation to the `MyAnnotation` class. It accepts an array of `@Attribute`
annotations that can be used to describe each supported attribute: the type of value that is expected,
and whether or not the attribute is required.

```
1   /**
2    * @Annotation
3    * @Attributes({
4    *   @Attribute("value", type="string", required=true),
5    *   @Attribute("hashMap", type="array<string>", required=false),
6    *   @Attribute("booleanValue", type="boolean"),
7    *   @Attribute("nestedAnnotation", type="MyAnnotation")
8    * })
9    */
10  class MyAnnotation
11  {
12      public $value;
13      public $hashMap;
14      public $booleanValue;
15      public $nestedAnnotation;
16  }
```

By default attributes are not required. When an optional attribute has not been provided, its value
will be `null`. When an attribute is of type `array` then the value that is provided will be converted to
an array automatically, so `"some string value"` becomes `array("some string value")`.

Validation using `@var` and `@Required`

The validation options provided by using the `@Attributes` annotation are very useful. But if you
don't like the fact that the rules for each property are not directly above that property's definition,
you can also choose not to use `@Attributes` and instead add type declarations for each property:

```
1   /**
2    * @Annotation
3    */
4   class MyAnnotation
5   {
6       /**
7        * @var string
8        * @Required
9        */
10      public $value;
11
12      /**
```

```
13        * @var array<string>
14        */
15       public $hashMap;
16
17       /**
18        * @var boolean
19        */
20       public $booleanValue;
21
22       /**
23        * @var MyAnnotation
24        */
25       public $nestedAnnotation;
26   }
```

To mark an attribute of the annotation as required, add `@Required` to the doc block above the corresponding property.

There is one nice option that adds a little extra to the validation process: the `@Enum` annotation. You can use it to define which values are allowed for a given attribute. This annotation has to be in the doc block of the relevant property. It works in combination with the `@Attributes` annotation as well as with the `@var` validation:

```
1   /**
2    * @Annotation
3    */
4   class MyAnnotation
5   {
6       /**
7        * @Enum({"yes", "no"})
8        */
9       $answer;
10  }
```

Now `@MyAnnotation(answer="yes")` would be valid, while `MyAnnotation(answer="unsure")` would trigger an error.

19.2 Limiting the use of an annotation

Different kinds of annotations have different use cases. For instance, the `@Entity` annotation from the Doctrine ORM does only make sense for classes, not for methods. On the other hand, the `@Template` annotation from the `SensioFrameworkExtraBundle` should only be used for methods, not for classes. Likewise, some annotations can only be applied to properties, like `@Type` from the JMS Serializer.

And some annotations can only be applied inside another annotation as one of its attributes, like the `@Attribute` annotation that can only occur inside an `@Attributes` annotation.

These different use cases are called "targets" and we can configure them ourselves per annotation class, by adding a `@Target` annotation to it:

```
1  /**
2   * @Annotation
3   * @Target("CLASS")
4   */
5  class MyAnnotation
6  {
7  }
```

The available targets are: CLASS, METHOD, PROPERTY, ANNOTATION and ALL (which is the default target for annotations if you don't specify it). If an annotation has multiple targets, you can provide them as an array of strings:

```
1  /**
2   * @Annotation
3   * @Target({"CLASS", "METHOD"})
4   */
5  class MyAnnotation
6  {
7  }
```

20 Valid use cases for annotations

You can do all sorts of things with annotations, but in my experience there are just a few valid use-cases for them.

20.1 Loading configuration

Most often annotations are used as a way to load static configuration for classes. These are some good examples of libraries that use annotations in this way:

- Doctrine ORM[1] for mapping entity types to database tables.
- Symfony Routing Component[2] for configuring routes in controller classes.
- Symfony Validator Component[3] for adding validation rules to any class.
- JMS Serializer[4] for configuring serialization options for any class.

In all of these libraries annotations are used as just a particular source of configuration. They all offer other, equivalent ways to accomplish the same thing, for instance loading some XML, Yaml or PHP configuration file. The result of loading configuration from all of these different sources will be used for the job at hand (preparing a database schema, validating or serializing an object, generating routes, etc.). In a way, annotations used for loading configuration are nothing special - they are just one of many ways.

An important characteristic of all these libraries that use annotations as a medium for configuration is that they only parse the relevant annotations once, and combine the results with data retrieved from other sources. The resulting data will be cached in order to make the second run much faster. After the first run, it does not matter anymore that the data originates from annotations, XML files, etc. The data has been combined and unified into one format.

Annotations and coupling

Some people complain that annotations increase class coupling. There are arguments for and against this position: annotations can be considered as "just comments", so they would definitely not increase class coupling, as class coupling is about how a class itself (not its comments) is coupled to other classes. However, when a doc block is being parsed, annotations are taken to be class names. So in this sense your class becomes coupled to the annotation classes it uses.

This special kind of coupling becomes very obvious when you have a class that has annotations for Doctrine ORM and for the JMS Serializer:

---

[1] https://github.com/doctrine/doctrine2

[2] https://github.com/symfony/routing

[3] https://github.com/symfony/validator

[4] https://github.com/schmittjoh/serializer

```
1   use JMS\Serializer\Annotation as Serialize;
2   use Doctrine\ORM\Mapping as ORM:
3
4   class Something
5   {
6       /**
7        * @ORM\Column(type="string")
8        * @Serialize\Type("string")
9        */
10      private $property;
11  }
```

Let's say that the project in which you want to use this class does not have the JMS Serializer as a dependency. But it does have Doctrine ORM and you want to use the mapping metadata to be able to store instances of `Something` in your relational database.

Well, as soon as Doctrine starts to read the annotations, it will fail, showing us the following error:

```
1   [Semantical Error] The annotation "@Serialize\Type" in [...] does not
2   exist, or could not be auto-loaded.
```

This is a very obvious sign that the `Something` class is indeed coupled to all of its annotations. Errors like these are the reason why you should not use annotations in a class when you want it to be reusable. When used outside the project, chances are it will fail because it misses a dependency.

Using annotations in classes that are only used inside one project seems fine to me (as discussed in another part of this book called Configuration conventions. There is no problem with that, since the class doesn't need to work in a different context.

20.2 Controlling application flow

Instead of being parsed just once, as part of some configuration loading process, annotations can also be used for influencing the flow on an application. The best examples are from the SensioFrameworkExtraBundle[5] which has annotations that control the way the `HttpKernel` eventually produces a response for a particular request. As explained in the first part of this book there are many points during that process at which event listeners are allowed to change the outcome. The `SensioFrameworkExtraBundle` contains multiple event listeners which will modify the `Request` object, create a `Response` object if none was returned from the controller, or modify a given `Response` object, based on the annotations that were provided in the doc block of a controller.

---

[5]https://github.com/sensiolabs/SensioFrameworkExtraBundle

For example, you can use the @Template annotation[6] above an action method in a controller class to indicate that the result of executing that action should be used as template variables:

```
1   use Sensio\Bundle\FrameworkExtraBundle\Configuration\Template;
2
3   class UserController
4   {
5       /**
6        * @Template("MatthiasAdminBundle:User:edit.html.twig")
7        */
8       public function editAction(User $user)
9       {
10          return array(
11              'user' => $user,
12          );
13      }
14  }
```

To make this work the SensioFrameworkExtraBundle registers an event listener which intercepts the kernel.controller event and collects @Template annotations for the current controller. It then tries to figure out which template file should be rendered and stores this file name in a request attribute called _template. When the controller has been executed and the return value is not a proper Response object, another event listener intercepts the kernel.view event and renders the template file mentioned in the request attribute _template using the return value from the controller as template variables.

---

[6]http://symfony.com/doc/current/bundles/SensioFrameworkExtraBundle/annotations/view.html

21 Using annotations in your Symfony application

As a PHP developer you are likely to write some library every once in a while that needs to load configuration from different sources, one of which might be annotations. If that is the case, then I'd like to recommend the jms/metadata package[1] to you. It provides some good tools that help you combine configuration (or "metadata") from different sources and store it as one object in a file cache.

I've written a few articles on my blog about using this library to collect metadata using annotations[2], to add an alternative driver for collecting metadata[3], and finally to cache the metadata properly[4].

In this chapter I choose not to discuss this subject in more detail, since the use of annotations for collecting metadata is not specific to Symfony applications. In fact, any application or library could make use of annotations in this way.

We will instead explore some ways in which you can control the application flow using annotations (the second use case). This subject was also partly covered on my blog some time ago in an article about preventing controller execution using annotations[5]. In the following sections I will describe a variety of other options that you have when combining annotations with kernel events.

21.1 Responding to Request attributes: the @Referrer annotation

Browsers have the useful habit to add a Referer header to a request (unless it is a direct request, like when you type a URL by hand or select one from your bookmarks). The name of the header actually contains a spelling error (it should have one extra "r": Referrer), but there's nothing we can do about that, except for making no spelling mistakes ourselves.

The Referer header contains the full URL of the page that was visited by the client before they requested the current URL. While handling a request you can use it to redirect a client back to where they came from. Or you could store the previous URL to later analyze which sites refer to your site.

In this particular example I'd like to use the Referer header to apply certain rules. For instance, some actions inside my application's controllers should only be executed when the user comes from a certain other page, and some of them are only available when the previous URL has the same domain as the current URL. Though this would not be a good security measure, it can be something

---

[1]https://github.com/schmittjoh/metadata

[2]http://php-and-symfony.matthiasnoback.nl/2012/03/symfony2-creating-a-metadata-factory-for-processing-custom-annotations/

[3]http://php-and-symfony.matthiasnoback.nl/2012/03/symfony2-writing-a-yaml-driver-for-your-metadata-factory/

[4]http://php-and-symfony.matthiasnoback.nl/2012/04/symfony2-metadata-caching-class-and-propertymetadata/

[5]http://php-and-symfony.matthiasnoback.nl/2012/12/prevent-controller-execution-with-annotations-and-return-a-custom-response/

that's nice to have. More importantly it is a good example of how you can influence the application flow based on an attribute of the current `Request` object.

 Be aware of security issues

Whenever you make your application logic depend on request attributes, think about any security issues that may arise from that. Some particular issues with request attributes are described in the chapter about [Security]{#request-attributes}.

Based on the scenario I described above, I should be able to write something like this above my actions:

```
1   class SomeController
2   {
3       /**
4        * @Referrer(pattern="^/demo", sameDomain=true)
5        */
6       public function specialAction()
7       {
8           ...
9       }
10  }
```

This would trigger some kind of validation mechanism which takes the `Referer` header and checks if its path matches the given pattern and if the referring URL has the same domain as the current URL.

The corresponding annotation class could look something like this:

```
1   namespace Matthias\ReferrerBundle\Annotation;
2
3   /**
4    * @Annotation
5    * @Attributes({
6    *   @Attribute("pattern", type="string"),
7    *   @Attribute("sameDomain", type="boolean")
8    * })
9    */
10  class Referrer
11  {
12      public $pattern = '.*';
13      public $sameDomain = false;
14  }
```

None of the attributes are marked as required. Instead I chose to add default values for the class properties $pattern and $sameDomain.

We want the referrer validation process to be triggered by an annotation that belongs to an action method of a controller class. What would be a good moment to do so? Well, as you may remember from the first part of this book: after the controller has been fully determined and resolved, the kernel dispatches a kernel.controller event. Event listeners are then allowed to do anything that's needed, given the current controller. This seems like a perfect fit. So in this case we should create an event listener that listens to this particular kernel.controller event. When the listener is notified of such an event, it can inspect the current controller and see if it has a @Referrer annotation.

The ReferrerListener below will do the trick. We'll make sure that its onKernelController() method will be triggered when a kernel.controller event is dispatched by the kernel. I assume that you know how to register this event listener.

```php
namespace Matthias\ReferrerBundle\EventListener;

use Doctrine\Common\Annotations\Reader;
use Symfony\Component\HttpKernel\Event\FilterControllerEvent;
use Matthias\ReferrerBundle\Annotation\Referrer;
use Symfony\Component\HttpFoundation\Request;

class ReferrerListener
{
    private $annotationReader;

    public function __construct(Reader $annotationReader)
    {
        $this->annotationReader = $annotationReader;
    }

    public function onKernelController(FilterControllerEvent $event)
    {
        // the current controller callable
        $controller = $event->getController();

        if (!is_array($controller)) {
            // we only know how to handle a callable that looks like
            // array($controllerObject, 'nameOfActionMethod')
            return;
        }

        // the annotation reader needs a reflection object like this
        $action = new \ReflectionMethod($controller[0], $controller[1]);

```

```
31        $referrerAnnotation = $this
32            ->annotationReader
33            ->getMethodAnnotation(
34                $action,
35                'Matthias\ReferrerBundle\Annotation\Referrer'
36            );
37
38        // $referrerAnnotation is either an instance of Referrer or null
39        if (!($referrerAnnotation instanceof Referrer)) {
40            return;
41        }
42
43        $this->validateReferrer($event->getRequest(), $referrerAnnotation);
44    }
45
46    private function validateReferrer(
47        Request $request,
48        Referrer $configuration
49    ) {
50        $actualReferrer = $request->headers->get('referer');
51
52        $pattern = $configuration->pattern;
53        $sameDomain = $configuration->sameDomain;
54
55        // do anything you like
56        // maybe throw an exception if you don't like it
57    }
58 }
```

Make sure that the service you create for this event listener will receive the annotation_reader service as its first constructor argument.

Annotations will be cached

When you depend on the Doctrine annotation reader, always type-hint to the interface `Doctrine\Common\Annotations\Reader`. Symfony itself uses `Doctrine\Common\Annotations\Reader\CachedReader` class which is an implementation of that interface. It is a proxy for the regular `AnnotationReader` class. The cached reader will cache the parsed annotations as serialized objects. In the case of a Symfony application those parsed annotations are stored in the `app/cache/{env}/annotations` directory. For example, the cached array of method annotations for the `specialAction()` method (see above) looks like this:

```
1   <?php return unserialize('a:1:{i:0;O:43:"Matthias\ReferrerBundle\Annotation
2   \Referrer":2:{s:7:"pattern";s:6:"^/demo";s:10:"sameDomain";b:1;}}');
```

21.2 Prevent controller execution: the `@RequiresCredits` annotation

In the following example I want to either prevent or allow execution of a given controller based on the amount of credits the current user has. Imagine that our application has some kind of credit system. The user can buy credits and then he is able to visit certain pay-per-view pages. For example: page A costs 100 credits. When a user has 150 credits, after visiting page A they have only 50 credits left. They will not be able to visit that same page again, unless they buy some extra credits.

I image it to look something like this:

```
1    class PayPerViewController
2    {
3        /**
4         * @RequiresCredits(100)
5         */
6        public function expensiveAction()
7        {
8            ...
9        }
10
11       /**
12        * @RequiresCredits(50)
13        */
14       public function cheapAction()
15       {
16           ...
```

```
17        }
18  }
```

First let's implement the corresponding annotation class:

```
1   namespace Matthias\CreditsBundle\Annotation;
2
3   /**
4    * @Annotation
5    * @Attributes({
6    *   @Attribute("credits", type="integer", required=true)
7    * })
8    */
9   class RequiresCredits
10  {
11      public $credits;
12  }
```

Then, just like in the previous example, we need to listen to the kernel.controller event and analyze the current controller and action, looking for a @RequiresCredits annotation to see if credits are required to execute this action:

```
1   namespace Matthias\CreditsBundle\EventListener;
2
3   use Matthias\CreditsBundle\Annotation\RequiresCredits;
4   use Matthias\CreditsBundle\Exception\InsufficientCreditsException;
5   use Doctrine\Common\Annotations\Reader;
6   use Symfony\Component\HttpKernel\Event\FilterControllerEvent;
7
8   class CreditsListener
9   {
10      private $annotationReader;
11
12      public function __construct(Reader $annotationReader)
13      {
14          $this->annotationReader = $annotationReader;
15      }
16
17      public function onKernelController(FilterControllerEvent $event)
18      {
19          $controller = $event->getController();
20
21          if (!is_array($controller)) {
```

```
22          return;
23        }
24
25        $action = new \ReflectionMethod($controller[0], $controller[1]);
26
27        $annotation = $this
28            ->annotationReader
29            ->getMethodAnnotation(
30                $action,
31                'Matthias\CreditsBundle\Annotation\RequiresCredits'
32            );
33
34        if (!($annotation instanceof RequiresCredits)) {
35            return;
36        }
37
38        $amountOfCreditsRequired = $annotation->credits;
39
40        // somehow determine if the user can afford to call this action
41        $userCanAffordThis = ...;
42
43        if (!$userCanAffordThis) {
44            // now what?
45            ...
46        }
47    }
48 }
```

Of course, the calculations that need to be made to calculate if the user can afford to visit this page should be done by a specialized service, to be injected as a constructor argument.

The question arises: what should we do next to prevent the HttpKernel from executing the controller when the user currently can not afford it. There are several different options here:

1. You can replace the current controller with another one, for instance a controller that renders a page where the user can buy some extra credits.
2. You can throw an exception, for instance an InsufficientCreditsException.

If you choose the first option then you should replace the current controller with a valid PHP callable. You could create a new controller on the spot, but it would be better to have it injected as a constructor argument:

```
1   class CreditsListener
2   {
3       ...
4       private $creditsController;
5
6       public function __construct(
7           ...
8           CreditsController $creditsController
9       ) {
10          ...
11          $this->creditsController = $creditsController;
12      }
13
14      public function onKernelController(FilterControllerEvent $event)
15      {
16          ...
17
18          // replace the current controller with another one
19          $event->setController(
20              array(
21                  $this->creditsController,
22                  'buyAction'
23              )
24          );
25      }
26  }
```

If you choose the second option, you could throw a custom exception, like this:

```
1   namespace Matthias\CreditsBundle\Exception;
2
3   class InsufficientCreditsException extends \RuntimeException
4   {
5       public function __construct($creditsRequired)
6       {
7           parent::__construct(
8               sprintf(
9                   'User can not afford to pay %d credits',
10                  $creditsRequired
11              )
12          );
13      }
14  }
```

```
15
16  class CreditsListener
17  {
18      ...
19
20      public function onKernelController(FilterControllerEvent $event)
21      {
22          ...
23
24          throw new InsufficientCreditsException($annotation->credits);
25      }
26  }
```

Just throwing an exception would result in the standard error page to be shown. Instead, you might want to customize the response for this particular exception. You can accomplish this by registering an event listener for the kernel.exception event. The event listener would receive a GetResponseForExceptionEvent object. It could then check if the exception that triggered the event is an instance of InsufficientCreditsException and if so, render a proper response for that exception, like a page where the user can buy some extra credits. It would look something like this:

```
1   use Symfony\Bundle\FrameworkBundle\Templating\EngineInterface;
2
3   class CreditsListener
4   {
5       ...
6       private $templating;
7
8       public function __construct(
9           ...
10          EngineInterface $templating // inject the "templating" service here
11      ) {
12          ...
13          $this->templating = $templating;
14      }
15
16      public function onKernelException(GetResponseForExceptionEvent $event)
17      {
18          $exception = $event->getException();
19          if (!($exception instanceof InsufficientCreditsException)) {
20              return;
21          }
22
23          $response = $this
```

```
24            ->templating
25            ->renderResponse(
26                'MatthiasCreditsBundle::insufficientCredits.html.twig',
27                array(
28                    'requiredCredits' => $exception->getRequiredCredits()
29                )
30            );
31
32        $event->setResponse($response);
33    }
34 }
```

Instead of returning a standard error page, the `HttpKernel` will return the `Response` object provided by the `CreditsListener`.

21.3 Modify the response: the `@DownloadAs` annotation

The last example in this chapter is about modifying the `Response` object based on a controller annotation.

When you want the result of a controller action to be offered to the client as a downloadable file, you have to do something like this inside your action:

```
1  use Symfony\Component\HttpFoundation\Response;
2  use Symfony\Component\HttpFoundation\ResponseHeaderBag;
3
4  class SomeController
5  {
6      public function downloadAction()
7      {
8          $response = new Response('body of the response');
9
10         $dispositionHeader = $response->headers->makeDisposition(
11             ResponseHeaderBag::ATTACHMENT,
12             'filename.txt'
13         );
14
15         $response
16             ->headers
17             ->set('Content-Disposition', $dispositionHeader);
18
19         return $response;
```

```
20        }
21    }
```

This is rather verbose and it is not good to have this type of difficult-to-read code inside every action that offers something for download.

Verbosity and repetitiveness in controller actions are often a sign that some of its functionality needs to be moved to a dedicated service. But sometimes it is a hint that the functionality might be pushed to an event listener instead, which does its magic at the right moment during the process of handling a request.

In this case it is safe to assume that creating an event listener would be the right thing to do. It would need to listen to the kernel.response event. This event is dispatched just before the Response object is handed back to the front controller, which is the right moment to turn the response into a downloadable file by adding the Content-Disposition header to it:

```
1   namespace Matthias\DownloadBundle\EventListener;
2
3   use Symfony\Component\HttpFoundation\ResponseHeaderBag;
4   use Symfony\Component\HttpKernel\Event\FilterResponseEvent;
5
6   class DownloadListener
7   {
8       public function onKernelResponse(FilterResponseEvent $event)
9       {
10          // we still need to determine the filename
11          $downloadAsFilename = ...;
12
13          $response = $event->getResponse();
14
15          $dispositionHeader = $response
16              ->headers
17              ->makeDisposition(
18                  ResponseHeaderBag::DISPOSITION_ATTACHMENT,
19                  $downloadAsFilename
20              );
21
22          $response
23              ->headers
24              ->set('Content-Disposition', $dispositionHeader);
25      }
26  }
```

If we would register this event listener right now, every response to every request would be offered as a downloadable file. This is not what we want. The response should only be a downloadable file if the controller action is marked as "downloadable". Let's do that by introducing a @DownloadAs annotation:

```
 1   class SomeController
 2   {
 3       /**
 4        * @DownloadAs("users.csv")
 5        */
 6       public function downloadAction()
 7       {
 8           ...
 9       }
10   }
```

We could implement the @DownloadAs annotation as follows:

```
 1   namespace Matthias\DownloadBundle\Annotation;
 2
 3   /**
 4    * @Annotation
 5    * @Attributes({
 6    *   @Attribute("filename", type="string", required=true)
 7    * })
 8    */
 9   class DownloadAs
10   {
11       public $filename;
12   }
```

Now we need a way to find out if the action that was executed has a @DownloadAs annotation. Unfortunately, inside the onKernelResponse() method we know nothing about the controller that was used to produce the response. This means that we have to hook into the process earlier, at a moment when we *do* know the controller. Again, the best thing to do would be to listen to the kernel.controller event and use the annotation reader to find out if it has a @DownloadAs annotation.

We can add another method to the DownloadListener class: onKernelController(). It should be notified of the kernel.controller event. We use the annotation reader to look for the @DownloadAs annotation. If such an annotation was found, we store the suggested filename as an attribute of the current Request object:

```php
1   use Matthias\DownloadBundle\Annotation\DownloadAs;
2   use Doctrine\Common\Annotations\Reader;
3   use Symfony\Component\HttpKernel\Event\FilterControllerEvent;
4
5   class DownloadListener
6   {
7       private $annotationReader;
8
9       public function __construct(Reader $annotationReader)
10      {
11          $this->annotationReader = $annotationReader;
12      }
13
14      public function onKernelController(FilterControllerEvent $event)
15      {
16          // this is more or less the same as in previous examples
17          $controller = $event->getController();
18          if (!is_array($controller)) {
19              return;
20          }
21          $action = new \ReflectionMethod($controller[0], $controller[1]);
22
23          $annotation = $this
24              ->annotationReader
25              ->getMethodAnnotation(
26                  $action,
27                  'Matthias\DownloadBundle\Annotation\DownloadAs'
28              );
29
30          if (!($annotation instanceof DownloadAs)) {
31              return;
32          }
33
34          // store the filename as a request attribute
35          $event->getRequest()->attributes->set(
36              '_download_as_filename',
37              $annotation->filename
38          );
39      }
40
41      ...
42  }
```

Don't forget to register this class as a service and register it as an event listener for both the `kernel.controller` and the `kernel.response` event.

Now when the controller for a request has been determined, the `onKernelController()` method of the `DownloadListener` class looks for a relevant `@DownloadAs` annotation, copies the filename from it and stores that filename as the `_download_as_filename` request attribute.

The only thing we need to do is to check inside the `onFilterResponse()` method if that same attribute has been provided. Only if it is, then the response should be available for download (i.e. have an "attachment" disposition), otherwise it will do nothing and return early:

```
class DownloadListener
{
    ...

    public function onKernelResponse(FilterResponseEvent $event)
    {
        $downloadAsFilename = $event
            ->getRequest()
            ->attributes
            ->get('_download_as_filename');

        if ($downloadAsFilename === null) {
            // the response should not be a downloadable file
            return;
        }

        $response = $event->getResponse();

        // set the content disposition
        ...
    }
}
```

22 Designing for reusability

Maybe you have noticed these similarities between the different event listeners that we have seen in the previous sections:

- All of the event listeners listen to the same event, i.e. `kernel.controller`. Only some of them listen to other events, like `kernel.response`.
- All of the event listeners require the Doctrine annotation reader to fetch annotations for a controller action.
- All of the event listeners only work when the controller is a callable defined as an array of an object and a method name.

This shared logic could easily be abstracted and this is something we should definitely do since it will make each of the event listeners much cleaner.

Let me just give my solution to this problem (like always there are different ways to accomplish the same thing):

```
 1  namespace Matthias\ControllerAnnotationsBundle\EventListener;
 2
 3  use Doctrine\Common\Annotations\Reader;
 4  use Symfony\Component\HttpKernel\Event\FilterControllerEvent;
 5
 6  abstract class AbstractControllerAnnotationListener
 7  {
 8      private $annotationReader;
 9
10      /**
11       * Return the class of the annotation that should be present for
12       * the current controller in order for the processAnnotation() method
13       * to be called
14       *
15       * @return string
16       */
17      abstract protected function getAnnotationClass();
18
19      /**
20       * Will only be called if an annotation of the class returned by
21       * getAnnotationClass() was found
22       */
23      abstract protected function processAnnotation(
```

```
24            $annotation,
25            FilterControllerEvent $event
26        );
27
28        public function __construct(Reader $annotationReader)
29        {
30            $this->annotationReader = $annotationReader;
31        }
32
33        public function onKernelController(FilterControllerEvent $event)
34        {
35            $controller = $event->getController();
36
37            if (!is_array($controller)) {
38                return;
39            }
40
41            $action = new \ReflectionMethod($controller[0], $controller[1]);
42
43            $annotationClass = $this->getAnnotationClass();
44
45            $annotation = $this
46                ->annotationReader
47                ->getMethodAnnotation(
48                    $action,
49                    $annotationClass
50                );
51
52            if (!($annotation instanceof $annotationClass)) {
53                return;
54            }
55
56            $this->processAnnotation($annotation, $event);
57        }
58    }
```

You can use this abstract class as the parent class for each event listener that acts upon controller annotations. For instance the ReferrerListener could become a lot cleaner once it extends from AbstractControllerAnnotationListener and correctly implements its abstract methods:

```
1   namespace Matthias\ReferrerBundle\EventListener;
2
3   use Matthias\ControllerAnnotationsBundle\EventListener\
4       AbstractControllerAnnotationListener;
5
6   use Symfony\Component\HttpKernel\Event\FilterControllerEvent;
7
8   class ReferrerListener extends AbstractControllerAnnotationListener
9   {
10      protected function getAnnotationClass()
11      {
12          return 'Matthias\ReferrerBundle\Annotation\Referrer';
13      }
14
15      protected function processAnnotation(
16          $annotation,
17          FilterControllerEvent $event
18      ) {
19          $actualReferrer = $event->getRequest()->headers->get('referer');
20
21          $pattern = $annotation->pattern;
22          $sameDomain = $annotation->sameDomain;
23      }
24  }
```

 ### No need to copy and paste this code

Because it would not make sense to copy this generic event listener class and paste it in each of the projects where you want to use controller annotations, I've created a small package for it: matthiasnoback/symfony-controller-annotation[1]. At the time of writing, this package only contains the abstract event listener class. If you have other needs, please open an issue or create a pull request on GitHub[2].

---

[1]https://packagist.org/packages/matthiasnoback/symfony-controller-annotation
[2]https://github.com/matthiasnoback/symfony-controller-annotation

23 Conclusion

Looking back at the examples above I think we may conclude that the use of annotations inside controllers is a great way to influence the application flow.

Controller annotations allow you to write domain-specific code in a higher-level language (the "annotation language"). The example of the `@RequiresCredits` annotation made this especially clear. It hides a lot of application logic from the user. Such annotations actually form domain-specific languages on their own. They make it easier for others to understand what is going on and allows them to implement the same thing faster, without copying and pasting complicated PHP code. This helps you prevent code duplication and promote reusability.

So next time you need a way to reuse part of a controller, ask yourself: is this a nice and justifiable use case for introducing a controller annotation? It will not take too much time to create a prototype for it if you use the `matthiasnoback/symfony-controller-annotation` package[1].

---

[1]https://packagist.org/packages/matthiasnoback/symfony-controller-annotation

VII Being a Symfony developer

Many of the developers that I know call themselves "PHP developer". Some of them might even say that they are a "Symfony developer". Others will say, "I am a developer", without revealing their favorite programming language or the only programming language they master.

When I started to work with Symfony, I almost immediately fell somewhat in love with this great framework. Its first version was already so much better than what I was used to. But the second version was just the right thing for my mind - I started learning a lot about it, digging deep into its code, writing documentation for parts that were still undocumented, writing articles about how to accomplish certain things with Symfony, and speaking in public about Symfony and Symfony-related PHP libraries.

After all of this, I would call myself a Symfony developer now. But the best part of the story is: everything that I learned from and while working with Symfony, is generally applicable to software written "for" any other PHP framework. Even when I work with a non-Symfony or a "legacy" PHP application (with no reused code at all), it still pays off to think about ways in which I can use code from the "Symfony ecosystem", or in fact, from any library that I can pull in using Composer, and make it a better application.

In this part I will demonstrate that being a good Symfony developer is about knowing the framework well, but then writing code that would be beneficent for any PHP project out there and finishing with a tiny layer between this code and the Symfony framework so that most of your code will be reusable even if it is being transferred to a non-Symfony project.

24 Reusable code has low coupling

24.1 Separate company and product code

Your situation as a Symfony developer is most likely:

- You are working for a company.
- You have customers (internal or external) for whom you create web applications.

When you start working on a new application, you will put your project's code in the /src direc-tory. But before you start, add two new directories inside this /src directory: /src/NameOfYourCompany and /src/NameOfTheProduct. Of course, these directory names should also be reflected in the namespaces of the classes you create for your project.

Whenever you start working on a new feature for the application - think of which part you could *in theory* reuse, and which part is unique for the application you are working on. Even when this reusable code will in practice *never* be reused, its quality will benefit from this mindset. Start developing classes in the company namespace. Only when you really feel the need to use something that is specific for the project, move it over to the product namespace, or use some kind of extension principle (a subclass, configuration, event listeners, etc.).

Writing reusable code for your company does not mean that it should be open sourced. It just means that you should write it *as if* it will be open sourced. You don't have to create side-projects for all the company code right away. You can develop it inside the project you're currently working on and maybe later make it ready for reuse in another project. Read more about the practical side of this in Dependency management and version control

 Coupling between company and product code

When you follow a strict separation between company and product code, this is a set of rules that help you make the separation really useful (when you don't follow these rules, there is no point in keeping separate namespaces actually):

1. *Company code* may know about or depend upon other *company code.*
2. *Company code* may *not* know about or depend upon *product-specific code.*
3. *Product-specific code* may know or depend upon other *product-specific* code.

The first two rules should be taken strictly into account: only when you do so, the code will ever be reusable or ready to be open sourced. The third rule on the contrary *adds* a lot of freedom: since you will by definition not reuse any product-specific code you are allowed to make it highly coupled to other product-specific code.

24.2 Separate library and bundle code

When you notice that you are writing classes and interfaces that have no relation with the entire Symfony framework, or only with some parts of the framework, you should separate your code into "library" code and "bundle" code. The library code is the part of the code that is more or less stand-alone (although it could have some external dependencies). Library code could be reused by a developer who works with the Zend framework, or with the Silex micro-framework (to name just a few). Bundle code replaces or extends some classes from the library code, adding extra Symfony-specific features. It defines a bundle configuration, and it has service definitions, to make instances of library classes available in the application. A bundle in this way just makes the library code available, while requiring just a minimum effort from developers who want to use the library in their Symfony project.

These are the things that belong inside a bundle:

- Controllers
- Container extensions
- Service definitions
- Compiler passes
- Event subscribers
- Container-aware classes that extend more generic classes
- Form types
- Routing configuration
- Other metadata
- ...

The list could be much longer. But it could also be much shorter. When you think about it, only the first couple of things on the list are really specific for bundles (i.e. used only in the context of a standard Symfony project). All of the other things could also be used in projects that only make use of specific Symfony Components. For instance form types could also be used in any PHP project with only the Form Component installed.

 Examples of library and bundle code

There are many good examples of this separation of bundle and library code. When you take a look at the code of Symfony itself, you can see this clearly: the directory `Component` contains all the Symfony components (the "library" code), and the directory `Bundle` contains the bundles which tie all the classes together, and provide configuration options which are passed as constructor arguments to all these classes. Many great examples of this strategy can be found in the `FrameworkBundle` (the "core" bundle: when it's present in a project, we call it a "Symfony project").

24.3 Reduce coupling to the framework

You can go quite far into reducing coupling to the Symfony framework or to one of its components, and thereby making your code even more reusable.

Event listeners over event subscribers

For example you should prefer event listeners over event subscribers. Event subscribers are special event listeners, that implement EventSubscriberInterface:

```
1  use Symfony\Component\EventDispatcher\EventSubscriberInterface;
2
3  class SendConfirmationMailListener implements EventSubscriberInterface
4  {
5      public static function getSubscribedEvents()
6      {
7          return array(
8              AccountEvents::NEW_ACCOUNT_CREATED => 'onNewAccount'
9          );
10     }
11
12     public function onNewAccount(AccountEvent $event)
13     {
14         ...
15     }
16 }
```

You can register event subscribers like this in a very clean way using the service tag kernel.event_-subscriber:

```
1  <service id="send_confirmation_mail_listener"
2    class="SendConfirmationMailListener">
3    <tag name="kernel.event_subscriber" />
4  </service>
```

There are some problems with this approach:

1. An event subscriber becomes totally useless when the Symfony EventDispatcher Component is not available, even though there is nothing Symfony-specific about this event listener.
2. onNewAccount() receives an AccountEvent object, but it is nowhere determined that such an object can only arise from an event with the name AccountEvents::NEW_ACCOUNT_CREATED.

Therefore an event listener which is actually an event *subscriber* is not good for reusable code. It couples the code to the EventDispatcher Component. It is better to remove the interface, remove the method required by the interface and register the listener methods manually using the service tag kernel.event_listener:

```
1   <service id="send_confirmation_mail_listener"
2     class="SendConfirmationMailListener">
3     <tag name="kernel.event_listener"
4       event="new_account_created" method="onNewAccount" />
5   </service>
```

Constructor arguments over fetching container parameters

When you know that the service container has just the parameter you need, it can be tempting to inject the entire container to just retrieve this specific parameter:

```
1   use Symfony\Component\DependencyInjection\ContainerInterface;
2
3   class SendConfirmationMailListener
4   {
5       private $container;
6
7       public function __construct(ContainerInterface $container)
8       {
9           $this->container = $container;
10      }
11
12      private function sendConfirmationMail()
13      {
14          $mailFrom = $this->container->getParameter('send_mail_from');
15
16          ...
17      }
18  }
```

The corresponding service definition would be:

```
1   <service id="send_confirmation_mail_listener"
2     class="SendConfirmationMailListener">
3     <argument type="service" id="service_container" />
4   </service>
```

This is obviously very bad for the mobility of this service: it can now only function when there is a Symfony service container available in the application. To make matters worse: even if there is such a service container, it is by no means certain that a parameter send_mail_from would be defined.

Therefore, always inject container parameters as constructor arguments, like this:

```
1  <service id="send_confirmation_mail_listener"
2    class="SendConfirmationMailListener">
3    <argument">%send_mail_from%</argument>
4  </service>
```

Constructor arguments over fetching container services

Just like fetching parameters from the service container directly, using the service container as a service locator is an equally bad idea.

```
1  class SendConfirmationMailListener
2  {
3      private $container;
4
5      public function __construct(ContainerInterface $container)
6      {
7          $this->container = $container;
8      }
9
10     private function sendConfirmationMail()
11     {
12         $mailer = $this->container->get('mailer');
13
14             . . .
15     }
16 }
```

The reason for doing things like this is usually performance. Say we would inject the mailer directly as a constructor argument:

```
1  class SendConfirmationMailListener
2  {
3      private $mailer;
4
5      public function __construct(\Swift_Mailer $mailer)
6      {
7          $this->mailer = $mailer;
8      }
9  }
```

Now, this class is an event listener and it listens to the new_account_created event. Whenever the listener gets instantiated, the mailer service will also be initialized, even when only in some cases a mail would be sent. This may take some time (and at least some system resources).

Though this is indeed true, injecting the service container to fetch a service is bad because:

1. It couples your code to a very specific type of service container (the Symfony service container).

2. The silent and possibly wrong assumption is that a `mailer` service exists (and that it is a `\Swift_Mailer` object).

3. Your service could fetch many more things from the service container than it should be allowed to.

The thing is: people get inspired to inject the service container from using the standard Symfony `Controller` class, which implements the `ContainerAwareInterface`. You basically should not use this interface nor its basic implementation `ContainerAware`. There are good use cases, but in most situations you really don't need the entire service container: you need *a specific service*. And your class should be coupled to this service's class or preferably its interface, not to the service container.

The performance issue

But what about the performance issue then? Well, since Symfony 2.3 you don't need to worry about that anymore. You can add the `lazy="true"` attribute to service definitions for which you want a proxy class to be created[1]. The result is that you can inject the real dependencies into your services, but they are only fully initialized when you call any of their methods for the first time. I created a small extension for this, the LazyServicesBundle[2] that allows you to make services lazy by pointing out (constructor) arguments that should be turned into lazy-loading services.

Framework-agnostic controllers

In Symfony applications controllers are usually the things that are most tightly coupled to the framework. When you always like to minimize coupling to anything (like I do), controllers seem therefore a good candidate to do so. We should however first consider the things that most controllers do when they are being executed:

- Take something from the *request* (either a route parameter, or a query attribute).
- Fetch some service from the *service container* and do the thing that was requested.
- Render a *template* with the variable retrieved from the service...
- Or add a *flash message* to the session, to notify the user of the result of the action...
- And *generate the URL* of some other page and *redirect* the user to it.

All of these things should be done in the way the framework expects you to do them. As you can imagine, this will make your controller very much coupled to the framework. *And it should be!* A Symfony controller would not function very well in another application which does not use the Symfony Router, the Symfony HttpKernel and the Symfony HttpFoundation components. And such an application I would like to call a "Symfony application".

So when it comes to controller classes you may skip any steps you would normally take to make a class decoupled. Therefore, don't be reluctant to extend your controller classes from the standard

---

[1]http://symfony.com/doc/current/components/dependency_injection/lazy_services.html

[2]https://github.com/matthiasnoback/LazyServicesBundle

Symfony `Controller` class. It will be very helpful since it provides many shortcut methods for things you often do inside a controller (e.g. `createForm()`, `generateUrl()`, `createNotFoundException()`, etc.).

Also, you don't have to define services for your controllers. They don't need to be reused *as* a service. However, I sometimes feel like it is a good idea to be able to take full control over the construction process of a controller, which would otherwise be instantiated "magically" using the `new` operator by the `ControllerResolver`, after which - also even more magically - the container will be injected, whenever the controller implements `ContainerAwareInterface` (read more about this in All the things a controller can be).

One last remark before you start happily coupling your controllers to the framework again: you should still try to make controllers as small as possible. When you enter the controller, you should quickly move the focus away from the controller to some kind of service that does the real work. See also Slim controllers for motivation and practical suggestions.

Thin commands

Writing a console command is very easy and generally recommended to provide ways to execute specific tasks for your bundle using the command line. But commands should be treated the same way as a controller gets treated: it should be a thin layer between the input the user provides, the services that are used to execute the task and the output that the user should receive about successes and failures.

Therefore, ideally, the `execute()` method of a command contains some checks on the input provided, and then immediately it fetches a service from the service container and calls some action on it.

```php
namespace Matthias\BatchProcessBundle\Command;

use Symfony\Bundle\FrameworkBundle\Command\ContainerAwareCommand;
use Symfony\Component\Console\Input\InputInterface;
use Symfony\Component\Console\Output\OutputInterface;

class BatchProcessCommand extends ContainerAwareCommand
{
    protected function configure()
    {
        $this->setName('matthias:batch-process');
    }

    protected function execute(
        InputInterface $input,
        OutputInterface $output
    ) {
        $processor = $this->getContainer()->get('batch_processor');
```

```
19
20          foreach (array('main', 'sub', 'special') as $collection) {
21              $processor->process($collection);
22          }
23      }
24  }
```

When you feel the need to do more things inside a command, move as many responsibilities as you can to specific services.

This again makes it easier to reuse command code, even with an entirely different library for executing commands. It also helps you to test the code that really "does things" better, since testing code inside a command is much more difficult and much less isolated than testing code in normal PHP classes.

Moving code away from the command class will make it more difficult to generate relevant output for the console. There is a perfect solution for this: use a bit of aspect oriented programming[3] to generate output based on the actual method calls and their return values.

The environment

Symfony has a very nice way of separating and cascading bundle configuration for different environments. These environments are called (by convention) dev, test and prod. This value is however entirely arbitrary. It is not even a class constant somewhere, but it's just the first argument used when instantiating the kernel in the front controllers in /web:

```
1  // in /web/app_dev.php
2  $kernel = new AppKernel('dev', true);
```

You should therefore never rely on the environment name or hard-code it inside any part of your code. Things like this must be avoided:

```
1  class SendConfirmationMailListener
2  {
3      private $environment;
4
5      public function __construct($environment)
6      {
7          $this->environment = $environment;
8      }
9
10     private function sendConfirmationMail()
11     {
12         if ($this->environment === 'dev') {
```

---

[3]http://php-and-symfony.matthiasnoback.nl/2013/07/symfony2-rich-console-command-output-using-aop/

```
13                    // always send the mail to matthiasnoback@gmail.com :)
14            }
15        }
16  }
```

Any modification of behavior depending on the environment of the application should take place on the level of your bundle's configuration and even then it should be implicit, since *which* environment names a developer uses is up to him, not up to you. In fact, when you copy everything from `config_dev.yml` to `config_prod.yml` your production environment will look and feel just like a development environment.

25 Reusable code should be mobile

The main characteristic of mobile code is that you should be able to take the code and easily transfer it to another application. After installing the code in another project, you know that it is mobile when:

- You can easily fix bugs in the code, even though the code has been duplicated many times.
- It does not fail because of another library, component, bundle or PHP extension that is *not* present in the other project.
- You can easily configure it to work with another database and maybe even another type of database.
- It does not fail because certain database tables or collections don't exist.
- It does not fail because it is placed in an unusual directory inside the project.

25.1 Dependency management and version control

The first two characteristics of mobile code are related to infrastructure: when reused, your code should not merely be duplicated - it should still be under version control so that each bug-fix can be easily distributed over the different copies of the code.

You can do this using a mechanism like externals, or sub-modules (depending on the type of version control software that you use), but the better way is to use Composer[1]. Each piece of code that you want to share between projects should be in its own repository. In case you want to keep the code for yourself (or for your company): host the repository privately, on GitHub[2], Bitbucket[3], etc. When you want to make your code open source, GitHub would be the currently fashionable place.

In both cases you need a composer.json file. This file will basically make your code known as something coherent: a *package*. In composer.json you can define the requirements (PHP version, PHP extensions and other libraries), you can instruct the autoloader on where to find classes and functions, and you can add some information about yourself, the package, and the tags it should have.

As an example: this is a somewhat modified composer.json from the knplabs/gaufrette library:

---

[1]http://getcomposer.org/
[2]https://github.com/
[3]https://bitbucket.org/

```
1  {
2    "name":          "knplabs/gaufrette",
3    "type":          "library",
4    "description":   "Library that provides a filesystem abstraction layer",
5    "keywords":      ["file", "filesystem", "media", "abstraction"],
6    "minimum-stability": "dev",
7    "homepage":      "http://knplabs.com",
8    "license":       "MIT",
9    "authors": [
10     {
11       "name": "KnpLabs Team",
12       "homepage": "http://knplabs.com"
13     }
14   ],
15   "require": {
16     "php": ">=5.3.2"
17   },
18   "require-dev": {
19     "amazonwebservices/aws-sdk-for-php": "1.5.*",
20     "phpspec/phpspec2": "dev-master",
21     "rackspace/php-cloudfiles": "*",
22     "doctrine/dbal": ">=2.3",
23     "dropbox-php/dropbox-php": "*",
24     "herzult/php-ssh": "*",
25     "phpunit/phpunit": "3.7.*"
26   },
27   "suggest": {
28     "knplabs/knp-gaufrette-bundle": "*",
29     "dropbox-php/dropbox-php": "to use the Dropbox adapter",
30     "amazonwebservices/aws-sdk-for-php": "to use the Amazon S3 adapter",
31     "doctrine/dbal": "to use the Doctrine DBAL adapter",
32     "ext-zip": "to use the Zip adapter"
33   },
34   "autoload": {
35     "psr-0": { "Gaufrette": "src/" }
36   }
37 }
```

The list of requirements should be exhaustive for all the core functionality of your package. When the package contains classes that can be used optionally, which require extra dependencies, mention them under suggest. When you have written tests for these classes (like you should) make sure to list these extra dependencies together with your testing framework under require-dev so that all tests can be executed by anyone and no test will fail or get skipped because of a missing dependency.

Package repositories

Whenever a repository has a composer.json in its root directory, you can submit it as a package on Packagist[4]. This will effectively make your code open source. When you don't want this to happen, you can also privately host a package repository using Satis[5]. This works great for sharing code over many projects in the same company.

After creating the composer.json based on what your code really needs, and registering it as a package, either using Packagist or Satis, you can install the package in any of your projects by running:

```
1   composer.phar require [name-of-package] 0.1.*
```

Now, your code also complies with the second characteristic of mobile code: after installing it, it will not fail because of missing or incorrect dependencies.

25.2 Hard-coded storage layer

Auto-mapped entities

One of the biggest problems with bundles out there is that some of them define entity classes (using for instance annotations) and then put them in the Entity directory inside the bundle. This automatically makes these specific entities available in your project. This may seem nice, but in most situations it is not: you are then not able to choose your own schema, add extra fields, or maybe leave out the entities entirely and redefine the model using, for instance, MongoDB.

When a bundle enforces a specific storage layer like described above, you will notice this as soon as you run a command like doctrine:schema:update: suddenly all kinds of tables are being created, beyond your control basically, since by enabling the bundle in which there are defined, these will automatically be registered. The same problem arises when you run doctrine:migrations:diff. Then a migration script will be generated for creating these tables that you never wanted in the first place.

Storage-agnostic models

The right way to define your bundle's model is to provide base classes. These base classes contain all the usual getters, setters and other methods for modifying or inspecting the state of an object. They have protected properties (instead of the usual private properties) with no mapping-related annotations at all. These *storage-agnostic* model classes should reside in the Model directory of your bundle, and they should not contain any code which is specific for their manager (like an EntityManager or a DocumentManager).

---

[4]https://packagist.org/
[5]https://github.com/composer/satis

```
1   namespace Matthias\MessageBundle\Model;
2
3   class Message
4   {
5       protected $body;
6
7       public function getBody()
8       {
9           return $this->body;
10      }
11  }
```

This allows developers who want to use your bundle to extend from the base class and define any metadata required for mapping the data to some kind of database in their own way:

```
1   namespace Matthias\ProjectBundle\Entity;
2
3   use Matthias\MessageBundle\Model\Message as BaseMessage;
4   use Doctrine\ORM\Mapping as ORM;
5
6   /**
7    * @ORM\Entity
8    */
9   class Message extends BaseMessage
10  {
11      /**
12       * @ORM\Column(type="text")
13       */
14      protected $body;
15
16      // Application specific data:
17
18      /**
19       * @ORM\Column(type="integer")
20       */
21      protected $upVotes;
22
23      /**
24       * @ORM\Column(type="integer")
25       */
26      protected $downVotes;
27  }
```

As you can see, this will also allow someone to add extra fields which are not defined in the reusable, generic model. Make sure your bundle has a configuration option for setting the user-defined model class:

```
1  matthias_message:
2      message_class: Matthias\ProjectBundle\Entity\Message
```

Model classes are library code (actually)

As suggested earlier you should move any code that is not specific for Symfony applications to their own libraries. The same applies to model classes. They should not be part of a bundle, but part of a library.

Object managers

Even when you have defined a storage-agnostic model, it does not mean that your entire bundle needs to be storage-agnostic. The only thing you need to take care of is that the users of your bundle should be able to implement their own storage handling and disable the standard way that you implemented. You can do this by applying the strategy pattern for loading exclusive services, and by making use of aliases.

Also, you should not forget to make the names of entity managers, document managers, etc. configurable. For instance Doctrine ORM allows users to define different entity managers for different entity classes. So even though the default entity manager is the right entity manager in most cases, you should add a configuration key for it in your bundle's configuration.

25.3 Hard-coded filesystem references

Make sure your bundle does not contain any hard-coded filesystem references outside* the bundle itself. You may assume that anything starting from the root of your bundle is in your control, but the location of the vendor directory, or the web directory, or any other directory should be considered unknown. In fact, they are: when it comes to the directory structure, nothing is fixed when using Symfony. There are only "sensible defaults".

Any reference you want to make to any file above ./ should be configurable in config.yml as part of your bundle's configuration. You may of course offer sensible defaults, so your bundle works out-of-the-box when installed in a standard Symfony project. The standard way to accomplish this is to define a scalar node in your configuration tree, with a default value. Then process the configuration in the load() method of your bundle's extension class and define a parameter for it. This parameter can later be injected, for instance as a constructor argument. See also Define parameters in a container extension.

Using the filesystem

When your bundle requires a location other than the database to store data, like uploaded files, consider making the bundle filesystem-independent. Since not every application has write-access to the hard disk of the server it is hosted on, you may choose to use a filesystem abstraction layer, like Gaufrette[6]. It has adapters for many kinds of filesystems (local or remote), and your services won't notice anything when you switch between them. There is also a GaufretteBundle[7] which further eases integration of the library with your Symfony bundles.

---

[6]https://github.com/KnpLabs/Gaufrette
[7]https://github.com/KnpLabs/KnpGaufretteBundle

26 Reusable code should be open for extension

Code that is reusable has to be flexible. A user of your bundle should be able to configure services in a different way than they were configured in the original project you developed it for. He should also be able to replace any service of the bundle with a custom implementation, without the entire system falling apart. In other words, reusable code should adhere to the principle "open for extension, closed for modification". The user should not be forced to change the original code, but only to replace or extend specific parts in order to better support his needs.

26.1 Configurable behavior

To make your bundle flexible, it should have a rich set of configurable options, with sensible defaults and information about what a certain option means. Only the services that are requested based on these configuration values provided by the developer in for instance `config.yml` should be fully loaded. See also the part of this book about Patterns of dependency injection. It contains many suggestions on how to make a bundle configurable.

26.2 Everything should be replaceable

By using a compiler pass (see also Patterns of dependency injection) it is possible to replace any previously created service definition with your own service definition, or to change the class or any argument of existing service definitions. This means that when a developer wants to replace part of the functionality of your bundle with his own, there will in theory always be a way to accomplish this. There are still some things that you have to do, to help developers with replacing just what they need to replace, while keeping other parts of the bundle unchanged.

 Many small classes, many single responsibilities

Most likely you share this experience with me: you have tried to use an open source bundle but you did not like part of the functionality offered by it. You tried to replace part of it, but this part got bigger and bigger until you almost developed your own bundle (and then you better *should* in my opinion!). The problem usually is that there is too little "separation of concerns" in such a bundle: some big classes try to do too many things. The lesson for you being:

- Write many small classes, with just a few methods and a single (conceptual) responsibility.
- Create many small services for these classes.

Use lots of interfaces

Define lots of interfaces for the classes that you use, both in your bundle and in the corresponding library code. Interfaces are literally the contracts that are signed between one object and another. A class that implements an interface says: don't worry about how I do things exactly, this is how you can talk to me.

A traditional example, using only classes:

```
1  class Translator
2  {
3      public function trans($id, array $parameters = array())
4      {
5          ...
6      }
7
8      ... lots of other methods
9  }
10
11 class TranslationExtension
12 {
13     private $translator;
14
15     public function __construct(Translator $translator)
16     {
17         $this->translator = $translator;
18     }
19
20     public function trans($id, array $parameters = array())
21     {
22         return $this->translator->trans($id, $parameters);
23     }
24 }
```

It has this service definition:

```
1  <service id="translator" class="...">
2  </service>
3
4  <service id="twig.extension.trans" class="...">
5      <argument type="service" id="translator" />
6  </service>
```

When a developer wants to replace the translator, he needs to extend from the existing Translator class to satisfy the constructor argument type-hinted Translator:

```
1  class MyTranslator extends Translator
2  {
3      ...
4  }
```

```
1  <service id="my_translator" class="MyTranslator">
2  </service>
```

But now `MyTranslator` inherits everything that is already in the `Translator` class, even though it is going to do things very differently.

A much better solution would be to define an interface for translators:

```
1  interface TranslatorInterface
2  {
3      public function trans($id, array $parameters = array());
4  }
```

The only thing a replacement translator has to do, is implement this interface:

```
1  class MyTranslator implements TranslatorInterface
2  {
3      public function trans($id, array $parameters = array())
4      {
5          // do things very differently
6          ...
7      }
8  }
```

Finally, any existing type-hints should be changed from `Translator` to `TranslatorInterface`:

```
1  class TranslationExtension
2  {
3      public function __construct(TranslatorInterface $translator)
4      {
5          ...
6      }
7  }
```

And now nothing stands in the way of replacing the existing `translator` service with the `my_translator` service, either removing the existing definition, adding a new definition, by changing the class of the existing definition or by defining an alias from `translator` to `my_translator`.

Cohesive interfaces

When trying to find out what methods really belong to an interface, strive for a coherent set of methods, that would definitely belong to any (future) class that implements the interface.

Use the bundle configuration to replace services

As I mentioned before, you could in theory replace everything there is in the service container by something you created yourself. There are many ways to do this. But they are all not so clean and they won't be good for maintainability. The best way I've seen so far is to allow other developers to replace specific services, by providing service ids through the bundle configuration:

```
1  # in /app/config/config.yml
2  matthias_message:
3      # point to a specific service that should be used
4      message_domain_manager: matthias_project.message_domain_manager
```

26.3 Add extension points

You can make behavior configurable, or allow others to replace parts of your bundle. But you can also add ways to extend the behavior of your bundle.

Service tags

One way to allow other bundles in an application to extend the behavior of your bundle, is to make use of service tags. You could think of the way you can register form types that can be used in the entire application:

```
1  <service id="address_type" class="...">
2    <tag name="form.type" alias="address" />
3  </service>
```

Using a compiler pass you can find all services with a given tag and do whatever you want with them. See also Service tags for implementation details and more examples.

Events

Events are great for allowing other parts of an application to hook into the execution of your bundle's code. You could use events to simply notify the system that something has happened:

```
1  $eventDispatcher->dispatch(
2      'matthias_account.account_created',
3      new AccountEvent($account)
4  );
```

Or you could use an event object to let other parts of the application modify (filter) some value, like the Symfony kernel itself does, when it dispatches its kernel events (see also Early response).

27 Reusable code should be easy to use

27.1 Add documentation

The Symfony Cookbook article about best practices for creating bundles[1] recommends writing documentation for bundles. The proposed format is Re-Structured Text[2] and the main entry point should be `Resources/doc/index.rst`. However, many PHP projects I know of also have a `README.md` file (which is in the Markdown[3] format), describing in a few words what the project is about and how to install it.

Documentation should cover at least:

- The main concepts in the design of your code.
- Use cases, illustrated with code and configuration examples.
- Service tags that can be used to extend functionality.
- Events that are being dispatched.
- Any flow-controlling exceptions[4] that can be thrown.

 Documentation for internal projects

When your bundle is going to be used only by your fellow developers, you should not expect them to read your documentation. They will just try to start using it, and you are in the same room with them, so they will just ask you if anything doesn't work as expected.

However, you still need to provide some documentation for internal projects, to prevent future problems in case you would accidentally or purposefully leave the team.

27.2 Throw helpful exceptions

Chances are that someone trying to use your bundle will encounter some problems. Maybe you forgot to make some requirements explicit, maybe you made some other assumptions about how and in what situation the bundle's services would be used. In order to help your "user" to overcome any problem in this area, you should throw helpful exceptions, which point him in the direction of the solution.

---

[1] http://symfony.com/doc/master/cookbook/bundles/best_practices.html

[2] http://docutils.sourceforge.net/rst.html

[3] http://daringfireball.net/projects/markdown/syntax

[4] http://php-and-symfony.matthiasnoback.nl/2012/12/prevent-controller-execution-with-annotations-and-return-a-custom-response/

Use specific exception classes

Choose your exception classes well, and preferably add some exception classes yourself:

```
1   namespace Matthias\ImportBundle\Exception;
2
3   class WrongFormatException extends \RuntimeException
4   {
5   }
```

This allows someone to catch exceptions from which the application may still be able to recover:

```
1   try {
2       $this->loadFile($file);
3   } catch (WrongFormatException $exception) {
4       // ...
5   } catch (FileNotFoundException $exception) {
6       // ...
7   }
```

Set detailed and friendly messages

There is a common misconception that you should not put all the relevant details in the message of an exception. This would be bad for "security". Well, since you should prepare your production environment to display no error messages at all, there's no problem in giving full disclosure in an exception message. On the contrary: you *should* provide all relevant details. So, use sprintf() to construct a nice and friendly message:

```
1   throw new \InvalidArgumentException(sprintf(
2       'Tag "%s" for service "%s" should have an "alias" attribute',
3       $tagName,
4       $serviceId
5   ));
```

In contrast with things like:

```
1   throw new \OutOfBoundsException('You are a hacker');
```

Which would communicate very clearly your opinion about the user, but not help a developer in finding out what he can do to prevent the error.

28 Reusable code should be reliable

28.1 Add enough tests

When your code should be stable and maintainable at any rate, it needs enough tests. What is enough? Maybe you don't need a 100 percent coverage, but at least the use cases that you *say* your code supports should be verified to work correctly using unit tests.

Writing the tests will not be such a difficult task, since when you followed my advice in the previous section, your bundle consists of small classes, and many of them have interfaces, so they should already be very test-friendly.

After you have tested the true units of your bundle, all the little classes in there, it is time to test them all together. In other words: write integration tests. In my bundles, this means most of the times manually instantiating some classes, prepare some constructor arguments and create some more objects, and finally run a single method on one of these objects (while keeping track of which is which). This step is important, as you want to find and fix any problems without going back to the browser after many hours of fast and furious coding in your favorite editor.

 Use a simple service container for integration tests

When you start writing integration tests, and you have indeed created many small classes that work together, the setup code for your tests may become quite large, with lots of new operators. To be able to reuse the setup code and to enhance its maintainability, you should consider using a simple service container like Pimple for managing the object graph that is required for your integration test. See also PHPUnit & Pimple: Integration Tests with a Simple DI Container[1].

Test your bundle extension and configuration

Something that is missing in the test suites of many bundles: unit tests for framework-specific classes like the `Bundle` class and, when applicable its `Extension` and `Configuration` class. You can usually skip the `Bundle` class, but the `Extension` and `Configuration` classes have logic that should be tested. After all, you want to make sure that all things inside your bundle are tied together correctly.

To test the bundle's extension class, you only need a `ContainerBuilder` instance. Then run the `load()` method of the extension and provide it with an array of config arrays:

---

[1]http://php-and-symfony.matthiasnoback.nl/2013/06/phpunit-pimple-integration-tests-with-a-simple-di-container/

```
1   namespace Matthias\AccountBundle\Tests\DependencyInjection;
2
3   use Symfony\Component\DependencyInjection\ContainerBuilder;
4   use Matthias\AccountBundle\DependencyInjection\MatthiasAccountExtension;
5
6   class MatthiasAccountExtensionTest extends \PHPUnit_Framework_TestCase
7   {
8       public function testLoadsDoctrineORMServicesWhenEnabled()
9       {
10          $container = new ContainerBuilder();
11          $extension = new MatthiasAccountExtension();
12
13          $configs = array(
14              array(
15                  'storage_engine' => 'doctrine_orm',
16              )
17          );
18          $extension->load($configs, $container);
19
20          $this->assertTrue(
21              $container->has('matthias_account.doctrine_orm.storage')
22          );
23      }
24  }
```

Configuration arrays

Please note that you have to provide an *array of arrays* as configuration values. This is the way application configuration works: the values can originate for instance from both config_dev.yml and config.yml. The configuration Processor merges these separate arrays into one.

Use the SymfonyDependencyInjectionTest library

Testing a bundle extension class (and compiler passes for that matter) will be much easier when you use the SymfonyDependencyInjectionTest[2] library. It contains base classes for your own PHPUnit test cases and custom PHPUnit assertions.

Testing the bundle configuration is mainly an exercise in testing the Config Component itself. But since the code in the Configuration class is itself configuration (think one second longer about that...), you need to make sure that this configuration is sound. This is how you can do it:

---

[2]https://github.com/matthiasnoback/SymfonyDependencyInjectionTest

```
 1   namespace Matthias\AccountBundle\Tests\DependencyInjection;
 2
 3   use Matthias\AccountBundle\DependencyInjection\Configuration;
 4   use Symfony\Component\Config\Definition\Processor;
 5
 6   class ConfigurationTest extends \PHPUnit_Framework_TestCase
 7   {
 8       public function testHasSensibleDefaults()
 9       {
10           $configurations = array();
11           $processedConfig = $this->processConfiguration($configurations);
12
13           $expectedConfiguration = array(
14               'user_types' => array('user', 'administrator'),
15               'send_confirmation_mail' => true
16           );
17
18           $this->assertSame($expectedConfiguration, $processedConfig);
19       }
20
21       private function processConfiguration(array $configValues)
22       {
23           $configuration = new Configuration();
24
25           $processor = new Processor();
26
27           return $processor->processConfiguration(
28               $configuration,
29               $configValues
30           );
31       }
32   }
```

 Use the SymfonyConfigTest **library**

Testing your Configuration class will be easier when you use the SymfonyConfigTest[3]
library. It contains a base class for your own PHPUnit test case and custom PHPUnit
assertions.

---

[3]https://github.com/matthiasnoback/SymfonyConfigTest

Conclusion

Though not from request to response, this has been quite a journey! I wrote the first pages of this book in April of 2013. In June I said it would take just 6 more weeks to finish it. Well, it took three months, but now it is exactly as I had imagined it to be: a book for developers familiar with Symfony, wanting to take an extra step. Now that you've finished the book, I hope that you found it interesting. And maybe you can use some of the practices described here in your work as a developer.

Since this is the last page of the book, it's time for some meta-comments!

I think that the PHP community has taken some huge steps in the last couple of years. There are some great tools and platforms now, like GitHub and Composer, Vagrant and Puppet. PHP developers are becoming aware of the commonality of their individual ideas (for instance as expressed by the PSR-* standards). They have also slowly started to take care of handling version numbers well (e.g. semantic versioning). And they are generally very much concerned about bugs in their open-sourced software (which other people use in production environments). Above all, many PHP developers contribute to open-source projects for free, which generates a good vibe and a great tradition of giving and sharing.

But PHP developers are not used to all of the activities related to working with or even delivering open-source software: defining a manageable list of package dependencies, distributing packages, releasing software to the world, announcing changes to an API, handling bugs reported by strangers, working with continuous integration, etc.

More importantly: developing software for reusability has proven to be quite a difficult task in itself. Luckily, there are many principles you can adhere to. Some of them are described in the last part of this book. And some of them are well known to people writing in other languages than PHP. See for instance the list of package design principles[4] as described by Robert Martin. Ideas like these are not known to everyone in the PHP community, while they should be. If I were to ever write a book again, it would be about that: PHP package design.

---

[4]http://butunclebob.com/ArticleS.UncleBob.PrinciplesOfOod

Made in the USA
Lexington, KY
27 April 2016